THE FUTURE IS MESTIZO

THE FUTURE IS MESTIZO
Life Where Cultures Meet, Revised Edition

VIRGILIO ELIZONDO

with a new Foreword by Sandra Cisneros
and Introduction by Davíd Carrasco

UNIVERSITY PRESS OF COLORADO

Published by the University Press of Colorado
5589 Arapahoe Avenue, Suite 206C
Boulder, Colorado 80303

The University Press of Colorado is a cooperative publishing enterprise supported, in part, by Adams State College, Colorado State University, Fort Lewis College, Mesa State College, Metropolitan State College of Denver, University of Colorado, University of Northern Colorado, University of Southern Colorado, and Western State College of Colorado.

The paper used in this publication meets the minimum requirements of the American National Standard for Information Sciences—Permanence of Paper for Printed Library Materials. ANSI Z39.48-1984

Library of Congress Cataloging-in-Publication Data

Elizondo, Virgilio P.
  [Avenir est au métissage. English]
  The future is Mestizo: life where cultures meet / Virgilio Elizondo.–Rev. ed.
    p. cm.
  Includes bibliographical references.
  ISBN 0-87081-576-8 (alk. paper)
  1. Elizondo, Virgilio P. 2. Catholic Church–Texas–San Antonio–Clergy–Biography.
3. Mexican Americans–Texas—San Antonio—Biography. 4. San Antonio
(Tex.)—Biography. 5. Mexican Americans—Ethnic identity. 6. Mestizaje–Texas–San
Antonio. I. Title.

BX4705.E454 A3 2000
282'.089'6872–dc21   99-059201

20 19 18 17 16 15 14   13 12 11 10 9 8

To BERNARD DESCOULEURS and his wife, Christiane, who first conceived of the idea of this autobiographical work, and to the Editors of MAME in Paris who saw the value of this work and first commissioned it.

To my good friend Professor Jacques Audinet, who has always been a constant source of support and whose restless, critical, and creative mind has always been a challenge ard an inspiration to me. Working with Jacques has always affirmed me in who I am, but challenged me to go beyond my own borders and limitations.

To my friends at the Institut Catholique, where I studied, the Jesuits at the *rue de Grenelle* residence, and the very good friends I made in Paris who made my stay in France such a memorable and profitable experience.

To my own family, who have always been a constant source of love and support. Without their constant backing, I would not have the tremendous security to take the creative risks of life that I have always enjoyed taking. And also to my extended family at the Mexican American Cultural Center and at San Fernando Cathedral, whose friendship, collaboration, and support give me the freedom to get involved in many creative endeavors.

To my archbishop, Patrick F. Flores, who has always been a source of support and inspiration in all my work.

To the many, many people — from boyhood neighbors to close friends from distant continents — whose support, confidence, and friendship have helped me to be the person that I am.

As a small token of my gratitude, I dedicate this book to all my friends and collaborators.

Contents

Foreword

On a recent flight to Chicago, breakfast arrived and I was both satisfied and amused to peel my foil packet and find on my tray scrambled eggs on a flour tortilla — a "breakfast burrito." The entire plane, businessmen and businesswomen, mothers with kids, grandparents and students, flight attendants and first class, was lifting breakfast burritos to their mouths and eating the food of my childhood, the food of my kitchen, *la comida de los pobres* at thirty thousand feet above the earth. I never thought I would witness such an absurd and wonderful event like this in my life — and on an airline named American, no less — but a lifetime, I have learned, is full of astonishments.

The *panza* perhaps is that country where we most often cross borders, reluctantly at first, with great trepidation and fear, sometimes accompanied by a coyote, but after the foreign becomes familiar, without a second thought. We become cross-cultural globe-trotters. In San Antonio, Texas, you only have to look at the Chinese-Mexican restaurants around town; "Wok a Mole" has to be my favorite name. Or how about the lovely *meztizaje* of tacos like fried wieners and scrambled eggs, or my grandfather's beloved peanut butter on flour tortillas.

So remarkable and amazing is living on la frontera that I like to compare it to living in a Fellini film. Where else could taxi cabs boast "San Antonio, All-American City," yet billboards tout canned beans as "Mega Bueno." Where else do the two languages of my childhood mix and merge and spark a new language, as when my bootmaker's wife found herself in the shop alone, faced with the task of using unfamiliar equipment to polish my boots. Not to worry, she quipped, *"Voy a hacerle el* try"— she was going to give it her all.

Where else but on *la frontera de la frontera* can one find Selena drag queens or tourist gift shops selling tire flower-planters? To be Chicano is suddenly chic. *Rascuache* becomes a mode of art, a lifestyle if you will, *trochemoche* an authentic San Antonio style of decorating.

I have suspected for a long time now that our job as Chicanos, as *mexico-americanos*, as amphibians, as citizens with one foot over there and one over here, is to be the bridge of unity, to be the translator in this new age, *el sexto sol*, this age of chaos in which we are living when one world ends and a new one begins. It is my belief that we artists are asked to be the visionaries, however crazy our ideas might at first seem. Father Virgilio Elizondo states that the mission of the mestizo is to create, and that the new humanity, the new culture is happening thanks to "the poets, the artists, the thinkers, the artisans." It is with this intent that Father Elizondo writes.

It is always, after all, about telling stories, stories that save our lives. I haven't thought about how someone in the priesthood could be walking a parallel *camino* as mine. So far had I removed myself from my Catholic upbringing that it hadn't occurred to me that my story of searching for a voice in American letters could also be the story of someone searching for his voice within the Catholic church, of finding strength from "otherness," and this otherness giving direction to one's work. We are both, in our own way, *haciendo el try.*

Like the Chinese *dicho*, we are blessed to be living in interesting times, on the border of the new *mestizaje*. As one member of this exciting *movimento* nudging and being nudged into the future, I am delighted to have discovered this book. I have seen the new millennium and the future is us.

—SANDRA CISNEROS
San Antonio de Bexar

Preface

The Great Border

I was born and raised on the west side of San Antonio and only once in my life have changed my permanent address — that was when our family store needed to expand and we moved to a new home a few blocks away. Today, I am the pastor of the parish in which my parents were married. San Antonio has always been my home.

In my very own town in the very lives of our people, the great border that has separated Mexico from the United States is being dissolved. In a natural and unsuspected way we are moving from division to synthesis and from separation to unity. Something quite new and unsuspected is taking place. It is as exciting as it is mysterious, as painful as it is joyous.

I suspect that those of us who live in San Antonio are too close to what is happening to really appreciate its magnitude. The more I have traveled to other parts of the world, the more I have discovered the uniqueness of what is happening at home.

During 1976–77 I temporarily migrated to Paris to work on a doctorate in theology. I frequently enjoyed the bistros and the brasseries around Saint Germain des Pres, Montparnasse, and Saint Michel. I did the serious research in the excellent libraries of Paris, but my most creative ideas came as I sat sipping on a *demi* of cold beer or a glass of the *Beaujolais village nouveau* and observing the incredible variety of people passing by on the street. It seemed as if the whole world were parading in front of me. Peoples from all the nations of the world were experiencing a universal city, a place where boundaries did not exist, where differences did not mean barriers. Could this city be symbolic of the future of our planet?

The Paris experience was especially meaningful to me because I had always lived on the frontier between two worlds: Mexico and the United States. I had not chosen to live there and neither had I migrated there. In San Antonio I felt at home among my own. Yet all my life I had felt pulled in two opposing directions — the U.S. way of life and the Mexican way of life. Sometimes I felt the pull would be so great that it would rip me apart. But I could not run away either to the United States or to Mexico, for both were as much a part of me as I was a part of them.

I often ask myself the question: Is the frontier between the United States and Mexico the border between two nations or is it the frontier zone of a new human race? The border between the United States and Mexico has been described by Octavio Paz, the great philosopher of Mexico, as the border between absolute otherness. It is not just the border between two countries, but the border between two humanities: between two worlds, two periods of time, two historical processes, two languages, two drastically different ways of life, two core cultural ideologies. The 3500 kilometers between the two countries is the political border between two nations, but it is much more. It is the meeting point and often the site of violent clash between two radically different civilizations.

Today, the borderlands between the U.S. and Mexico form the cradle of a new humanity. It is the meeting ground of

ancient civilizations that have never met before. Old cultural
borders are giving way and a new people is emerging. No
one is planning it, but it is happening. It is not a political
question or an economic one; it is the human question of life
itself as it is emerging on a planet rapidly becoming smaller
and smaller.

In the Southwest of the United States, the North of planet
earth is meeting the South, and the result transcends old barriers by fusing North and South into a new synthesis. In this
portion of the earth, differences are not destroyed, hidden, or
ignored; they are absorbed to become the active ingredients
of a new human group. The borders no longer mark the end
limits of a country, a civilization, or even a hemisphere, but
the starting points of a new space populated by a new human
group. To be an intimate part of the birth of this *nueva raza*
is indeed a fascinating experience.

I am one of this race and the pains and joys of this new
existence are the core of my daily life. This new race is not
a theory or an ideology, but a living reality in the making.
I do not propose to create it but merely to understand the
dynamics of what is happening. And as a human being who
is somewhat aware of the contemporary situation of the multiple migrations at all levels of society and in all directions, I
ask myself what is the future of our planet? Furthermore, as
a Christian, I pose the questions: how can I best live out the
gospel in the midst of these particular circumstances? Can
the gospel show me a way to help build a world in which "all
may be one"? Does the gospel have something to say to the
pressing questions of today's shrinking planet?

San Antonio, Texas, by reason of its history, location, and
present-day population, is one of the urban centers where
the new humanity is emerging and taking shape. It is the
history alive today in the people of San Antonio that creates
the collective soul for this new group on planet earth. This
soul is the foundation and guiding force of the new expression

of the cosmic race made up of Nordics and Latins, Europeans and Natives, Africans and Asiatics — not merely co-existing but together exhibiting the new *rostro y corazón* (countenance and heart) of the new people of the globe.

Introduction

The Future Is Mestizo:
We Are the Shades

by Davíd Carrasco

We are entering the Brown Millennium. By Brown Millennium I mean the type of hopeful and complex change summoned by the poet Paul Celan when he wrote

> Speak
> But keep yes and no unsplit
> And give your say this meaning
> Give it the shade

No more the color line as the only defining symbol of race and culture in this country. No more the border line as the primary defining political scar between Latin America and the United States. Latinos are speaking with voices and living lives that combine criticism and affirmation of the United States and ourselves. We say "no" to the debilitating provincialisms of the white/black discourse and "yes" to the potentials of the new *mestizaje* of democracy. Latinos are the "unsplit." We are the shades! The

Brown Millennium that Latinos represent extends to include all people because with the influx, input and involvement of Asians, Africans, Europeans, and Latin Americans into the complex interactions of the global city and especially the United States, the overall hue and cry will be shades of brown, black, white, red, and yellow.

Or in the words of the prophet Virgilio Elizondo, the future is mestizo. In order for the future to favor a new knowledge of measured inclusions and not nullifying provincialisms, love and not hate, then a new order of meaning of what mestizaje is and is becoming must emerge in our minds and cultural practices. Elizondo is a prophet of mestizaje in the face of the troubling and horrible trends of ethnic cleansing and vicious narrow-mindedness. I am referring not only to the ethnic cleansings of the Balkans but the massacres of American Indians, the deportations of Mexican Americans, the enslavement of African peoples. Elizondo, the priest-theologian-activist from San Antonio, is not a "New Ager" but a "new thinker" and he focuses on the creative power of the new mestizaje, the Brown Millennium. While politicians, businesspeople, and the media freeze our sense of the future with hysteria about "Y2K," Elizondo, speaking as a Chicano, says something like "*porque y2k? y que?*" The real challenges and opportunities of the future are not only in computer systems, but also in developing a real knowledge of ourselves, biologically and spiritually. This involves for Elizondo, first of all, acts of cultural and spiritual memory. Writing of the new model of human existence that emerges from the Mexican-American experience, he refers to a dialogue in which he has been involved during his pilgrimage through Mexico, Holland, France, Japan, and the United States:

> The more we talked and explored the destructive status of our world, the more we became convinced that our USA-

Latino mestizaje was the greatest thing we had to offer the human family! Not the mestizaje of Latin America which had produced such a deep sense of shame in everything Indian and such an over exaggeration of everything European, but the new mestizaje which we Hispanics are discovering and elaborating here in the USA—one that joyfully reclaims the heritage of all our parents, grandparents, and ancestors. A denial or even worse a shame of one's heritage is a life of eternal self-torture and self-destruction. A reclaiming and restructuring is a life of freedom and creativity. This is the mestizaje we long to introduce to others and offer its fascinating benefits for humanity.

The second move in Elizondo's future beyond memory is critique—critique of Anglo supremacy and the stultifying white-black discourse that has dominated and obsessed cultural work in the United States for centuries. Latinos are the shades of culture, race, labor, and religion that set the stage for a new order of meaning about the power and nature of democracy in the twenty-first century. We know that Latinos will be the largest minority in the United States within two decades. This means that the new demography can be a creative resource for a new democracy. On the one hand, Elizondo and I are grateful and inspired by the lessons and gifts of the multiple ways that the black struggle for freedom has renewed our democracy. Latinos need to continually draw strategies and wisdom from the multiplicity of ways that African Americans have widened the doors of opportunity for peoples of color. But we are also impatient with the tenacity and provincialism of the reduction of race, culture, and humanity to white and black categories. I recently experienced this impatience when going by an "Amistad" window—one of those store windows promoting the movie *Amistad*, which depicts the story of the rebellion of African slaves on the high seas and their long struggle for freedom from slavery and human degradation in this country. In this window there were books and a few articles about the film and the controversies and lawsuits associated with it. I noticed an unusual weariness and anger in my response—tired of something in yet another Hollywood depiction of the white/black world. I did not feel amistad/friendship toward the film version of this story, and this bothered me. I had to examine myself and this weary anger and I explored three possible causes. First, I asked myself if the relentless market forces pushing this story of white-on-black atrocities in my face caused my discomfort. These market forces are colossal, monumental, and some of my discomfort stemmed from the market as manipulator. But I knew the problem was deeper than that.

Second, I had to ask a harder question. Did I detect some latent racism in me? This is always a possibility in a society where children are saturated with racial nullifications—mostly against people of color but today against all people. I examined this possibility because I had grown up with a father who was the first Mexican American to be a head basketball coach at a major university in this country and who brought the first African American athletes into public view in college basketball in Washington, D.C. In those days, Georgetown University, the University of Maryland, George Washington University, and Catholic University only recruited and played white basketball players in their public games. As a young boy, I had been on the playgrounds at Spingarn, Dunbar, and Kelly Miller schools and knew firsthand what it was to combine educational justice with athletic competition. This was a rare story in which a Chicano was crossing the color line by enabling black athletes to do the same. Still, I had to monitor the possibility of negative racial feelings at the window. Latinos need to check themselves on this point because more often than not, Latin Americans who come to this country feel the pull of expressing or adopting superior racial feelings promoted by traditions of white superiority. In actual fact, Latinos are multi-racial and many are black or have had decades-long positive interaction with African Americans and share soulfulness. It is crucial, as the Puerto Rican cultural critic Juan Flores argues, that in the Brown Millennium Latinos not embrace the media-hyped ascendency of non-black elements of Latino society at the expense of us all. But this was not the problem I experience with *Amistad*.

No, what was wearing me out and causing some rising anger was the interpretive power of the Spielberg version of the black/white dichotomy—here symbolized in the Spanish word *amistad*, meaning "friendship." As the white/black discourse has become mulitlayered and commercialized, it has also become an agent of exclusion of the many emerging narratives of race and class in the history to the United States, or the struggles, oppressions, cultural traditions, and creative engagements of Latino peoples. The social and racial complexity and dynamism of black-red-white-Latin American relationships, in the hands of the mainstream media, is becoming less visible, not more so. This growing exclusion was wearing me out and bringing some rumble to my humble. I was fed up with seeing films about color line relations that erased the past that was mestizo but also threatens to marginalize the future that is mestizo, even though Latinos have often been right in the middle, in the gravity of American stories.

This tenacious hold to the "color line" interpretation of history is being loosened by the expansion of mind represented in this book. Certainly the color line will continue to be one of the problems of the twenty-first century but, as Elizondo states, we are really facing a century of borderlands. We are moving beyond the color line and it is Mexicans, Puerto Ricans, Cubans, Guatemalans, and others who are the living beyond. The hybrid is crossing the color line, and bridges are being built that lead to a compelling question spoken by the Puerto Rican word artist Mária Fernández (*aka* Mariposa): "What does it mean to live in between?"

The third move in Elizondo's vision, after memory and critique, is a new vision of the borderlands that we all inhabit. The borderlands are moving in all directions from the south, and they bring democracy's fullest hope and deepest challenges because we are the shades. The borderlands have shades! They move from sharp, crooked lines into thick cities. We do not inhabit or cross only the borderlands of the Rio Grande or what Puerto Ricans call *el charco*, the Caribe. These borders have never been stable—they have always immigrated! Our relations with the United States teach us that it is not only Latin Americans who immigrate into the Untied States but also the U.S. borders that move and invade! The U.S. borderlands moved south in 1848 after the Mexican American War to include California, Arizona, New Mexico, Texas, and parts of Colorado and Utah. The U.S. border moved again in 1898 to engulf Puerto Rico in an annexation that is still in hot dispute. As Father Elizondo says, "I'm not an immigrant. My family has lived in the San Antonio Valley before this country was country. So it is for many Latinos. We didn't come to you. You came to us."

Now the borderlands are moving again as Spanish, Portuguese, and Creole languages, food, literature, art, family patterns, religious faiths and imaginations, sexual fire, musical heat, myths, athletes, and ideas migrate north and spread out in all directions. One advertiser calls us "Mega Bueno." The real borderlands that I am speaking about are cities: Los Angeles, the great linguistic, social and racial borderlands that is the capital of the Third World; New York, about which someone said recently, "the good thing about New York City is that it is so close to the United States." In his new book *La Memoria Rota*, ("broken memory,") Puerto Rican cultural critic Arcadio Diaz Quinones shows us that New York has been, in part, a Caribbean city for over one hundred years. A city blessed with such Caribeños as José Marti, Celia Cruz, Eugenio María de Hostos, Machito, Tito

Rodriguez—and we now hear the bomba, plena, and salsa sounds in all Puerto Rican immigrant neighborhoods from Lorraine, Ohio, to Hartford, Connecticut, from Perty Amboy to Hawaii. Other cities of the Brown Millennium are Miami, the city on the edge; Denver, the city in the air; Boston, the city that is green once a year; San Juan, the city in the painful sea; San Francisco, the city of Barrio Mission and Dr. Loco and the Rockin' Jalapeño Band; El Paso, the city of the violated outrage where the old gringo of Carlos Fuentes made his fateful crossing and the farm workers make theirs. El Paso and the Mexican American border have moved up to Chicago. And so on and on.

When I speak of the Brown Millennium and Elizondo says the future is mestizo, we mean that the United States is entering the fuller recognition that it is a world of racial, cultural, and political shades. The many-hued, multicolored America—with Asian, Latin American, African peoples mixing, enriching and challenging our democracy—will be neither a black world nor a white world. What Elizondo and I are asking of our black brothers and sisters is how can we remake democracy together when the mestizo hybrid crosses the color line, which has been one of the great problems of the twentieth century? Juan Flores puts it well when he writes, "cultural expression in all areas—from language and music to literature and the visual arts—typically illustrates fusions and crossovers, mutual fascinations and emulations, that have resulted in much of what we identify, for example in the field of popular music, as jazz, rock and roll, and hip-hop. . . . And this conjoined cultural history put the lie to any wedge driven between latin@ and black life and representation." How can we work together for justice and equality when Latinos join African Americans as the most creative minority in the United States? What happens when the claim that *the* color line is the narrative space from which to remake democracy becomes a zigzag, a salsa step, a cumbia move?

Let me make it clear by the Brown Millennium I do not mean just the expanded Latino presence, but that the overall hue, shades and meanings will be mestizo. The Chicano artists called Culture Clash recite this perspective when they tell of someone killed in the Mission District in San Francisco the following. Speaking to us from heaven says

But Who was I while I was Alive
Was I a Man
A Woman
Was I Cop
I don't remember
I said to myself, I'm an American
And in that same precious instant I said
What is an American
I don't remember
The population of heaven is young and brown
Does not Speak English
I found very few Americans here
In fact everyone here seemed to be black, Latin or Chinese
So I guess heaven was like Earth
And the Mission district was becoming more like heaven every
   day

We ask our white brothers and sisters, "What happens to your power and privilege when, in the lifetime of any twenty-year-old college student, you will live in a society where no one ethnic group, including whites of European descent, will comprise a majority of the national population. How will you respond when policies and attitudes of white supremacy undergo yet another sustained critique? Can you live with the shades?"

We are asking everyone in the new future that is mestizo to give us some shades in the new democracy.

give us some shades

I ask us all—can we turn the new demography into a new democracy? What does it mean for our future language of democracy when we discover that more African American peoples speak Spanish and Portuguese in the Americas than speak English? Do you realize that Spanish is also an American language—a language spoken in the America one hundred years before English was heard on these shores?

What do we say in the face of the recent conflict in an East Palo Alto school board meeting where a black parent yelled at Latino parents, "If you want to learn Spanish, why don't you go back to Mexico?" Is that like me saying, "If you want to celebrate kwanzaa, go back to Africa"? Both positions are unacceptable in the Brown Millennium.

And why do some think that democracy can only be spoken in English? I agree with Doris Sommer, who "defends code-switching as one of democracy's most effective speech-acts, along with translation and speaking English through heavy accents, because they all slow down communication and labor through the difficulties of understanding and reaching agreement." Slow down in the Brown Millennium.

Can we forge a critical amistad? A critical friendship that will help Latinos go to school on the black struggle for freedom and help blacks and whites go to school on the more complex history of race, race discourse and mixture of Latin America. The new knowledge that Elizondo calls us to may allow African Americans to confront and find powerful new positive meanings in their mestizaje and enable whites to pull back the masks of purity that protect and inhibit their own fuller humanity. Some years ago, the great writer Ralph Ellison ended his novel *Invisible Man* with the critical question, "Who knows but that, on the lower frequency, I speak for you?" Well, it may be hard to take at first, but Elizondo is answering back, "In part, yes, and thank you brother, but in fact and in future, who knows but that on all frequencies we speak for and with all of us." The reader will have to decide how far Elizondo has gone in this book toward articulating a creative balance between diversities and inclusions while respecting differences and accentuating what we share. In the words of his new essay in this book, "I can become infinitely more creative for I have more cultural words within me than anyone who is a descendent of only one culture. I can even have more fun for I can party in many more ways than imagined by any one group alone."

What I ask of all who read this and celebrate and learn from *The Future Is Mestizo*

is
give us some shades
for together
we are the future and shades of democracy.

In the thought of Elizondo this means knowing the worst that we all have done and can still do but also seeking with all our hearts, minds, and bodies, the best of each and all of us. Give us some shades on the future that is mestizo.

THE FUTURE IS MESTIZO

Chapter 1

A Family of Migrants

My City

I am a middle-aged priest working in San Antonio — a city of a very rich and complex cultural make-up. With a few minutes drive from one area of the city to another, you can easily imagine yourself in an early colonial town of New Spain with its gardens and beautiful churches, in a small German village clustered around a flowing stream, or in a French convent with its Benedictine arches and hallways.

Walking through the streets of San Antonio, you easily recognize the native faces of the present-day descendants of the Apache, Comanche, Chichimeca, and other pre-Columbian inhabitants of this land. They are not extinct nor living on reservations. They form part of the complex organic mosaic that makes up this city on the great frontier between the United States and Latin America.

You need not go far in San Antonio to encounter blacks — descendants of the Africans who were brought in as slaves; in many cases their socio-economic lot has not improved much since the days of slavery.

But most of all, it seems as if you are in Mexico. The smell of spices, *carne asada, menudo,* and *tamales* permeates the area; the sound of Mexican music is heard all around. If

1

you hear English occasionally, it seems as if it is being spoken by a tourist from a distant country. In the churches, the sound of ancient *alabados** is heard combined with the trumpets and guitars of modern *mariachi* music. During the times of the great religious festivals, you will be easily absorbed into the folk-rituals of *las posadas* at Christmas or *la procesión de las tres caídas* on Good Friday. In the midst of the tenth largest city of the U.S. the experience is like being in a distant land in another period of history. The political boundary may be two hundred miles away, but socially and culturally speaking much of San Antonio is still in Mexico — or, as some people say, that part of Mexico presently occupied by the United States.

Many of the people of Mexican ancestry did not migrate to the United States. From the time the Spaniards arrived in the 1700s, they mingled with the natives and thus gave birth to the original Texans. They were already living in San Antonio and its surrounding area when the first immigrants from the Eastern shore arrived. They too fought for the independence of Texas. But when Texas was annexed to the United States, they quickly found themselves to be foreigners in their own country, exiles who never left home.

Even when Texas became part of the United States, people from Mexico continued to come — not to "another country" but simply to the other side of the river. For the masses of the poor in Mexico, Texas still appears to be part of their land. The United States may occupy it, but the land belongs to the people, to the native inhabitants and to their *mestizo* descendants. Hence, regardless of the laws, they freely come and go within what they consider their homeland. No civil law will ever change this for the law of the *carnalismo* of the land is much deeper and more persistent than any law made by civil authorities.

---

*Songs with Spanish lyrics and ancient Indian melodies

And the Mexican influence continues to expand. More and more advertisements in Spanish are seen throughout Texas. The Spanish International Television network is growing. Spanish-language radio stations continue to multiply. Spanish is used as the ordinary language in more and more churches. No priest would be named bishop of San Antonio if he were not fluent in Spanish. The richly decorated and simple-flowing dresses of the Indian women are becoming the ordinary dress for more and more women of fashion. Politicians are careful at least to greet the people in Spanish. Mexican food such as *tacos, flautas, gorditas, chalupas, enchiladas, tamales,* and an endless list of other delicacies have captured the American heart and become as American as ice cream and apple pie and are even displacing the traditional steak and potatoes as the great American food.

Today, the mayor of San Antonio, the Catholic archbishop, the chief of police, and many of the leading merchants and community leaders are Mexican-American. Yet this does not mean discrimination has come to an end. Racism continues to flourish in many subtle and not so subtle ways — in real estate, in education, in job opportunities, in the world of finances.

The city is criss-crossed with ultra-modern highways — almost symbolic of the many international routes that lead the inhabitants of many lands to San Antonio. Not only is it a bilingual city where Spanish and English are used equally in the streets, in business, and in worship, but there is even a new language being born: Spanglish — a unique and colorful blending of English and Spanish. Will this be the language of the Americas of the future? I think it is already happening.

My Family

I was born and grew up within a community of migrants and long-time residents who as far as I can remember never thought of themselves as migrants. We were at home in land that had been illegitimately taken by Yankee immigrants who, having become Mexican citizens, then turned around and betrayed the country to which they had pledged allegiance. As children, we never looked upon them as heroes or freedom-fighters, but as land-hungry swindlers who came to Mexican-Texas for the precise purpose of taking it over for themselves. Even the Texan-Mexicans who had fought together with the Yankee immigrants against the bad government of General Santa Anna had in the end found themselves to be equally defeated. It turned out that the battles had not so much been against bad government as against Mexico and Mexicanity.

I remember very well one of the old grandmothers whose ancestors had always lived in the San Antonio area telling us: "When the Spaniards arrived hundreds of years ago, we welcomed them and taught them how to survive in these hostile lands, and pretty soon they dispossessed us. Then came the immigrants from the United States, and the same thing happened. We don't know what country will be coming through here next, but we will still be here!" For many of the people in this region there is no memory of migration, but there is an experience and memory of having been colonized. We have never left the land, but the land has been taken away from us. We have never chosen to leave our homes, but many of our people are homeless. Whether our families have been here all the time, or whether we have simply come from the other side of the river (a popular way of saying we have come from the other side of the border), there is a deep sense of being at home — *en nuestra tierra.*

My parents owned and operated a small grocery store, which was not only a family business but which, along with the local Catholic church, was the center of community life and exchange of news. The women would take their time doing the shopping, while the men waited in the backyard drinking beer, exchanging "men stories," and telling good jokes.

Everyone knew each other by name and had a sincere interest in the needs and goings-on of people in the neighborhood. Many of the customers not only bought from us, but would help with the cleaning up and other aspects of the business. If my father wanted to go fishing, he would simply close the store and go. If the fish were biting, he would bring back plenty to give away to everyone. If he didn't catch any, we would have a lot of good stories to tell about the ones that got away. The store was hard work, but it was fun.

We had a small home, which was shared by my parents, my sister and me, my mother's mother — Doña María Manuela Petra Paula Ester Fernández del Castillo viuda de Peimbert — my father's father — Don Antonio — three canaries, two cats, and two beautiful German police dogs named Kaiser and Tarzan. It was a simple home — no hot water, a wood stove, and an old ice-box. Today it would be unthinkable. Yet in those days, we were not aware that we were missing anything. Besides, my grandmother was an accomplished cook and not only did we never lack for a good meal, but there was always extra food for an unexpected visitor.

Looking back, I can see that we were not rich or even middle class, but we never lacked anything, especially a lot of personal care and affection. If my mother got after us for something, my grandmother was always around to console us and spoil us. There were always neighborhood kids around and the whole neighborhood was one big extended family. Materially we did not have much, but socially we were most fortunate. We never looked upon ourselves as deprived of anything. In fact, I think we were truly of a privileged class — one in which tender, loving concern was the ordinary rule of the day and in which hard work was intermingled with many good times.

My parents were both immigrants from Mexico. My father had come from a very large and very poor family in the small town of Rosales in Northern Mexico. At the age of thirteen, he had been sent to San Antonio to seek out an uncle who had a grocery store so that he could work there and send some money home. In those days there were no trains or buses in that region of the country. My dad did not know any English whatsoever and he was walking into totally unknown lands. He walked and asked for rides and gradually traveled the more than 200 miles of near desert lands under the blistering sun of Texas. Even that he arrived is a small miracle in itself. Similar stories continue today as thousands of poor people struggle to escape the disastrous conditions of Mexico and Central America.

My father never had much schooling, but he was gifted with wisdom and practical know-how. He never went beyond the third grade, yet I have never met a more educated man. He had a gift for sizing up the situation and making a quick practical conclusion. He could add numbers just by looking at them much quicker than someone else could with an adding machine.

He endured many hardships — long working hours, poor living conditions, harsh treatment because he was a working nephew and not one of the sons of the family. Yet the hardships did not embitter him or dampen his enthusiasm. Life was never easy for him but he did not allow the struggles for life and survival to dominate him; rather he dominated and conquered them. His constant sense of humor and his great generosity toward those in need are still legendary among those who knew him. He was a very good businessman and could have become rich quite easily if he had wanted to, but instead he chose to love life and live it to the fullest.

My mother came from a totally different setting. She had been born of a very wealthy family in Mexico City. Their family home was a thirty-six room mansion in the most fashionable section of Mexico City. My great grandfather had immigrated from France and my grandfather had been a very successful engineer in Mexico City. The family had enjoyed the life of leisure of high-society Mexico until all tumbled to a quick end with the unexpected death of my grandfather. Those were not the days of insurance policies and my grandmother knew absolutely nothing about her husband's business.

Those were also the days of great political turmoil in Mexico. Governments were changing every few days and were consistently troubled by the revolutionaries who were passing through. My grandmother was a young widow with two beautiful young daughters living in a huge mansion in Mexico City. She had no money to support herself although the home gave the appearance of great wealth. They had dropped from wealth to poverty overnight. Luckily, her older sister had married a *norteamericano* — a man from the United States — who was willing to bring my mother and grandmother with him to the United States. They were fortunate, yet it was still difficult. An incredible and unimagined new life of hardships and joys awaited them in the new land of opportunity.

Working was so much below the dignity of the high-class ladies of Mexico, but there was no choice. So my grandmother started to work and my mother continued her education in a Catholic college for young women. My mother never forgot when one of the nuns asked her to give her class work to one of the wealthy girls in the class because the wealthy girl's parents would never understand her low grade! Those who had little or nothing were to give what little they had to those who already had too much. That seems to be the unwritten law of so many civilizations: the poor work hard to make it easy for the rich to reap and enjoy the rewards of the efforts of the unfortunate.

My mother quickly got a job as a secretary, but it wasn't easy to go from a carefree existence in Mexico to the demanding life of a legal secretary in the United States. My mother has always expressed gratitude for the patience of the first Anglo lawyers who hired her and patiently worked with her as she struggled with legal terminology in a language she was just beginning to learn. Yet she had the determination to succeed and she became an excellent secretary.

My parents met at a Tuesday Night Dance Club, and after a few years they decided to get married. All their friends thought they were crazy. Those were the Depression years. They didn't have any property, any money, and apparently any future. Yet, love has reasons that reason will never be able to reason to. So they started. It was the union of two very unlikely persons — for my mother and father were totally different. Yet, as far as I can remember, they made a perfect match. I have never known a more loving and more caring couple. One of my greatest treasures is the memory of this love and concern of my parents for one another and together for their family. In them, I saw and experienced the unlimited love of God.

My father never learned English well, but that was never an obstacle to his ability to communicate effectively in either English or Spanish. He developed a good business and the respect of everyone. He would easily walk right past the secretaries into the manager's office of any of the places we did business with and was proud of his good credit rating at the Frost Bank, San Antonio's leading bank. In time, he helped to start the first bank owned by Latins: The West Side State Bank — "West Side" having a pejorative connotation in San Antonio since it is the district in which the poorest Mexicans live.

If he had inferiority complexes or painful memories about his past, I was not aware of them. He was a hard worker, a deeply religious man (though not churchy) and very dedicated to the betterment of *nuestra mexicanidad* within the United States. He loved the United States because of the liberty and free spirit that reigned here. Yet he would get very upset at the gross stereotypes that the people of the United States had about Mexicans. He became a proud and loyal citizen of the

U.S.A., but this did not mean he wanted to cease being who he was. Our Mexican background and language were always regarded as a treasured honor — never to be forgotten for the sake of our new civic identity.

My mother always had the ability to be a good listener. Doña Anita not only helped run the store, but she helped people in the organizing and running of their lives. It seems that there were always school kids from the neighborhood visiting with her. She would spend time with kids from broken homes, encourage school drop-outs to return to school, tell young girls how to be proper *señoritas,* and build a sense of self-pride in all the kids who visited her. Many of the salesmen would come by more to visit with her than to get orders. She was the neighborhood psychologist. Many of the professionals around San Antonio today remember that it was she who consistently made them feel good about themselves and encouraged them to keep working hard at school to succeed. It is amazing how many people around San Antonio had good wisdom to share because of what they received from her.

My sister, like myself, always brought many friends around the house. Our home served as the community recreation center, for our friends were always around. I don't remember ever getting bored or lonely. When we were not working in the store, we were playing in one way or another. We had great childhood games that served as a natural initiation into the whole process of life.

I always admired my sister very much although I hated the fact that she didn't have to study to make good grades while I had to slave through the books merely to make a passing grade. In the early years, studies always appeared so boring. She has talents that I would love to have, but don't. She is an excellent artist and musician. Today her works of art can be found on exhibit around the country.

My early home memories would not be complete without a mention of my grandmother. Her life and example have been one of the deep and lasting influences on my life. She lived a simple existence, like what you would expect of a pious monk. She had a very simple room and never dressed in fancy clothing. I don't remember ever seeing any jewelry on her. Her time was spent in prayer, visiting from her window with anyone who passed by, or in the kitchen fixing the noonday meal. The odors that came from the kitchen still make my mouth water today. She was a true artist of the kitchen.

But what I remember the most was her philosophy of life. She was one of the happiest women I have ever met. She radiated inner peace, serenity, and happiness. She used to say that the greatest gift God had given to her was having taken everything away from her. In my younger years, this did not make any sense, since I always wanted to have more things. Yet in time, it made more and more sense to me. In Mexico, she had had great material comforts. Yet in losing material wealth, she started to discover deeper things in life. In the simple but joy-filled existence of our home-store in San Antonio, she had discovered the true things that were worth living for. She had, in effect, discovered the mystery of life.

My Neighborhood and Parish

For all practical purposes, our neighborhood could have been a small town in Mexico. Everyone spoke Spanish. The occasional English-speaking person passing through the neighborhood always seemed to be an oddity. We were all Catholics and the few Protestants around seemed to be from another planet.

The only institution in the area that was clearly Anglo-Saxon-Protestant-U.S.A. was the public school, where all the teachers were from another part of town and of course non-Spanish-speaking. The school grounds were like a little island of the U.S.A. within Mexico. There, the kids were forbidden to speak Spanish and even punished for doing so. While at home we heard about the Alamo traitors, at school they were presented as the Alamo heroes. Much later on in life, I was to learn that there are various versions of history — all true, but no one of them exhaustive. The ones that appear as traitors to one are the heroes of the other. The freedom-fighters of one side are the terrorists of the other.

But in my own first experiences of school, I was very fortunate. My parents sent me to the parish kindergarten operated by Mexican nuns, the Cordi Marian Sisters. It was simply an extension of the home. The sisters did their shopping in our grocery store as did the parish priests. They frequently visited our home, and all the families from the area felt welcome in the convent and kindergarten. We not only had school, but dances, plays, games, and all kinds of activities. We had a wonderful experience of belonging.

The local parish was always full of activity. Sunday mass was but one of the many activities that attracted us to the parish. Before the days of television, the parish had weekly movies — cowboys and Indians, detective, romance. Sometimes they were in Spanish and other times in English, but they were always great fun. The many novenas, processions, crownings, and special devotions kept us all entertained. Church was the best circus anywhere. We loved it. The church was the center of life. It was the community living room where we all met and enjoyed each other. From birth and baptism to the last anointing and funeral it permeated our lives and gave us the experience of being a united family. Because of this early experience, I love to think of the church as the great circus that is the gathering place of fools and clowns — for is it not true that the wisdom of God is foolishness to men and women of this world and that we are called to be fools for Christ? It is a refreshing and life-giving image: the great circus of God's people.

I can thank those early days around the church for developing my taste for good wines. The parish priests were from

Spain and they always had excellent Spanish wines for mass. They did not seem to be disturbed by the fact that the mass wine seemed to evaporate very fast in the sacristy — as the altar boys got an early start in wine-tasting. It was one of the rewards for serving at the altar. Maybe that is what started my vocation to the priesthood!

During my boyhood days there were no questions whatsoever about my identity or belonging. We grew up at home wherever we went — playgrounds, school, church. The whole atmosphere was Mexican and there were no doubts in our minds about the pride of being Mexican. Radio stations provided us with good Mexican music and the local Mexican theaters kept us in contact with the dances, folklore, romance, and daily life of Mexico. The poverty of Mexico, which was always evident in the movies, was completely surpassed by the natural simplicity, ingenuity, graciousness, and joy of the Mexican people. The United States was so efficient, but Mexico was so human. The contrasts were clear. We might be living outside the political boundaries of Mexico, but Mexico was not outside of us. We continued to interiorize it with great pride.

Como México no hay dos — there is nothing else like Mexico. Being Mexican was the greatest gift of God's grace. We loved it, lived it, and celebrated it. In many ways, we felt sorry for the peoples who were not so lucky as to be Mexican. In those early years I never thought of myself as a native born U.S. citizen of Mexican descent. My U.S. identity was quite secondary to my Mexican identity. Yet I was happy living in the U.S.A. We belonged to this land called the United States and this land belonged to us. In those early days, I never experienced being Mexican as not belonging. This was my home. I was born here and I belonged here.

Little did I think in those early years that the foundations of a new identity were already being formed within me. I was living a new identity that had not yet been defined and that would take many years to emerge. The new identity was beginning to emerge, not as a theory of evolution or as a political ideology of one type or another. It was rather a life lived not just by me, but by thousands of others who were living a similar experience. We were the first of the new human group that was beginning to emerge.

Chapter 2

Who Am I?

Moving into a "Foreign Land"

The paradise existence of the neighborhood came to a halt the first day I went to a Catholic grade school operated by German nuns in what had been a German parish. There the pastor still told Mexicans to go away because it wasn't their church. My parents had sent me there because it was the nearest Catholic school. Mexicans were tolerated but not very welcome.

The next few years would be a real purgatory. The new language was completely foreign to me and everything was strange. The food in the cafeteria was horrible — sauerkraut and other foods that I only remember as weird. We were not allowed to speak Spanish and were punished when we got caught doing so. The sisters and lay teachers were strict disciplinarians. I don't think I ever saw them smile but I remember them well hitting us frequently with a ruler or a stick. They were the exact opposite of the Mexican sisters around our home who were always happy, joking, and smiling and formed us carefully through counsels, suggestions, and rewards. In one system we were punished for the bad things we did while in the other we were rewarded for our good accomplishments.

Mass was so different. Everything was orderly and stern. People seemed to be in pain and even afraid of being there. It was a church of discipline, but it was not one of joy. In fact, joy seemed to be out of place. Mass was recited, not celebrated. People went because they had to, not because they wanted to. It seemed like a totally different religion.

It was hard going to school in a language that was almost completely unknown and in surroundings that were so foreign and alienating. Things did not make sense. I used to get very bored. The school hours seemed eternal; the clock appeared not even to move during those horribly unintelligible hours. My parents had to force me to study and it was very difficult for me even to make passing grades. Going to school was so different that it was like crossing the border every day, like going to another country to go to school, even though it was only a few blocks from our home.

It was during these days that I first started to get a feeling of being a foreigner in the very country in which I had been born and raised. Guilt started to develop within me: why wasn't I like the other children who spoke English and ate sandwiches rather than *tortillas?* I started to feel different and mixed-up about who I was. But the mixture and the bad feelings came to a quick end every day at three o'clock when school was dismissed and I returned home. It was the beginning of life in two countries that were worlds apart.

I wanted to become what I felt I had to be, for it was my parents, whose authority and wisdom I never questioned, who had sent me to that school. Yet it meant not so much developing myself as ceasing to be who I was in order to become another person. Those three years in primary school were awful. I was afraid to mix with the kids and often felt better going off by myself. The teachers were constantly getting after me for day-dreaming. That was my natural escape mechanism or, better yet, my instinct to survive. The dreams were my spontaneous efforts to create an existence of my own, thus refusing to accept the existence that was being imposed upon me.

As I look into the past and try to understand it from my present perspective many years later, I re-experience the original pain, sadness, embarrassment, ambiguity, frustration, and the sense of seeking refuge by being alone. Yet I can also see that it was already the beginning of the formation of the consciousness of a new existence — of a new *mestizaje.** The daily border crossing was having its effect on me. I didn't know what it meant. I didn't even know why it had to be. But that constant crossing become the most ordinary thing in my life. In spite of the contradictions at school, there was never any serious doubt in my mind that my original home experience in a Mexican neighborhood was the core of my existence and identity; there my belonging was never questioned. There I did not seek to go off by myself but was developing into quite an outgoing person.

Acceptance, Belonging, and Affirmation

By the time I was ten, my parents moved me to another school in downtown San Antonio. It was the old German school called St. Joseph's. There things started to change for me. I ended up with a teacher who was a German-American from an Alsatian congregation — Sister Michael Rose. She was one that combined demanding discipline with lots of love and understanding. She always had the most beautiful smile and even when she had to correct us she did it in such a way that she never put us down. She was stern but friendly; she was interested in our family life and took a personal interest in each one of her students. For the first time, a teacher of

---

**Mestizaje:* the process through which two totally different peoples mix biologically and culturally so that a new people begins to emerge, e.g., Europeans and Asians gave birth to Euroasians; Iberians and Indians gave birth to the Mexican and Latin American people.

another nationality was not a distant other. She was a friend. That made all the difference.

All of a sudden, school started to be exciting. I actually stayed after school hours to help the teacher and do extra work. The old contradiction between home and school was not present — or maybe I had simply gotten used to it and had started to assimilate it. I made new friends of various ethnic backgrounds and enjoyed running around with them after school hours.

But walking around the downtown area every day brought some new experiences. I started to discover blacks. Before, I had never even known about their existence. Those were still the days of segregation when the blacks had to sit in special "colored balconies" in the theaters, attend black churches, sit in the back of the public buses, and use separate toilets in public places. Many of my school friends had darker skin than myself and I remember well the problems we experienced just trying to go to the toilet. If we went into the one marked "colored" we were chased out by the blacks because we were not technically black. Yet, we were often chased out from the ones marked "white" because we had dark skin. So we didn't even have toilets to which we could go. Our being was actually our "non-being." This consciousness of "non-being" would deepen and broaden as I gradually moved from a very secure experience of being, to one of non-being, to one of new-being.

The schools had done a good job of convincing us that we were different, but the schools were trying to help us be ordinary and like everyone else. They did not say we were different or inferior in so many words, but they did not have to. All the courses indicated this by pointing to the Anglo-American models of existence as the only normal existence of intelligent, civilized human beings. How could we want to be otherwise? To be otherwise was backward, underdeveloped, somewhat stupid — that is, inferior.

During these early years, I realized more and more that I could easily adjust to the Anglo-American ways of the U.S.A., yet there was never any doubt that my family was *puro mexicano*. We prided ourselves on everything Mexican. One of the most fascinating days in the life of the entire neighborhood was when the Mexican soccer team came to play in San Antonio and defeated the U.S. team. It was as if Mexico had conquered the U.S.A. We were jubilant with joy and pride.

We did not attempt to define what it meant to be Mexican. We did not have to. We knew who we were and we were proud and happy to be just that. With equal degrees of certitude we knew we were not Spaniards, we knew we were not Indians, and we knew we were Mexican. We did not go into our origins, but simply loved and celebrated our existential identity. If the U.S. was the land of opportunity and development, Mexico was the land of ancient civilizations, sophisticated culture, and beautiful customs and traditions. The U.S. had a great future; Mexico had a great past.

My first visit to Mexico City was like going to the very navel of our existence. I anticipated it like going to heaven itself. My grandmother had always told us stories about the grandeur and beauty of Mexico. When we arrived, my uncle, aunt, and cousins took us around and truly feasted us. Riding on the *chalupas* — small flat boats — through the ancient pre-Columbian canals of Xochimilco was a thrill — like being in contact with the original waters of creation, like going through a cultural baptism, a rebirth, a reaffirmation of life.

But nothing can surpass my first visit to the Basilica of Our Lady of Guadalupe. It was like entering into the womb of life. I did not then nor do I now have adequate words to explain it all. It was awesome but inviting. It was sacred, but so human — people all around, praying, doing sacrifice, visiting, eating, pick-pocketing. All of life was present there. It attracted people like a huge magnet. There was constant movement of people coupled with the permanence of the *Vir-*

gencita. The people's faces exhibited resignation and expectation, pain and joy, disappointment and fulfillment, fatalism and struggle, history and dreams, yesterday and tomorrow being celebrated today. This was Mexico. This was and is Mexicanity! Here, in the presence of *nuestra madrecita morenita* — our brown-skinned mother — everyone was!

Experiences of Non-Being

Yet this certitude of being Mexican began to be questioned whenever we visited our relatives in Mexico. Even though they loved us and we loved to visit them, in many ways they would let us know that we were *pochos* — Mexicans from the U.S.A. To this day, it is not uncommon to hear someone in Mexico say about a Mexican-American's Spanish, "For a *norteamericano,* your Spanish is not so bad." Yet it is not uncommon for an Anglo-American from the U.S. to say about a Mexican-American speaking perfect English, "For a Mexican-American your English is pretty good." Whether in Mexico or the U.S. we are always the distant and different "other." The core of our existence is to be "other" or to "not be" in relation to those who are. Yet being called *pocho* in Mexico was not insulting, for we were fully accepted. There was always rejoicing when our families visited us in San Antonio or when we visited them in Mexico. *Pocho* was simply a reality. Even though the U.S. was our home, it was in Mexico that we felt more and more at home. The label marked distance and difference but not separation or rejection.

This was an experience totally different from being called "Meskins," "Greasers," or "wetbacks" in the U.S.A. The titles were used to remind us that we were different — meaning that we were backward, ignorant, inferior, scum. We were not wanted in the U.S., merely tolerated and exploited. Our people were consistently subjected to multiple injustices. The movies depicted us as treacherous bandits or drunken fools and our women as wanting nothing better in life than to go to bed with one of the white masters. Anglo-American society had no doubts that it alone was the Master Race! Indians, Mexican half-breeds, and blacks were inferior and therefore to be kept down for the good of humanity.

It was bad enough that the Anglo society projected this imagery, but what made it even worse was that many of our people believed it. As kids, the worst insult was to see young Anglos come by and easily pick up the Mexican-American girls while the young men were left standing around. Maybe this explains why many of the Mexican-American militant leaders of the 1960s and 1970s married Anglo women, especially blondes.

I lived on the border between two nationalities. I was an inside-outsider to both. I was "Mexican" in the U.S. and *gringo/pocho* in Mexico. There was a painful side to it, for it is difficult to always be different, but there was also an enjoyable side to it; I had a lot more options and could move easily in and out of two worlds. For as much as I loved the Mexican side of me, I never really disliked or hated the Anglo side, which I was making my own in the schools. Yet it was painful and incomprehensible because there were so many Anglo racists. Since I loved and admired Mexico so much the only conclusion I could logically come to was that the racists were ignorant. Much later on, I would discover that it was not just ignorance, but the Anglo drive to dominate, subjugate, and exploit. And even when some Anglos wanted to be of help, it was by helping the other become like themselves.

I loved visiting Mexico, but I always knew that I would never live there. The United States was my home, it was my country, it was my nationality. My parents had also come to the decision that they would never return to live in Mexico. At first they had dreamed of returning to retire in Mexico. But as time went on, they were proud and happy to live in the United States. Without ever despising the Mexican in us, each day we appreciated more and more the advantages and the opportunities of the U.S. way of life. It was just painful that the *rubios* (blonds) did not like us and often looked down upon us in many ways. And in spite of the many positive aspects of life in the U.S. "American culture" seemed to be so rude; people always shouted at one another, interrupted each other, drank too much Johnny Walker.

High school was a good time for me. The teachers were very strict and demanding, but always showed concern and respect for difference and individuality. I attended a private military school where nothing half-way was tolerated. If we did not turn in our assignments on time, we got a whipping in front of the whole class and then we were allowed to give our excuse. As they always told us, it is results that produce, not excuses.

Although I hated school and even failed in the early grades, during my high school years I moved to the top of my class, never making anything less than "A." It was in high school that I felt totally accepted and respected simply for being who I was. There I did not even think of being Mexican or American. I was allowed and encouraged to be. By this time, I had pretty well mastered English but prided myself in keeping up good Spanish. I could not imagine the possibility of not speaking Spanish. It was part of my soul.

My college years at St. Mary's University in San Antonio proceeded in much the same manner. I decided to major in chemistry and biology. It was quite a challenge since these were among the most difficult subjects in the curriculum. Many times I had to stay up all night to complete my assignments. I not only survived, but did well. The faculty, made up largely of a religious congregation of men, were fine professors and always very encouraging. Many of my teachers, Brothers of the Society of Mary, became close friends and visited my home often. They quickly became part of our extended family.

But college was not all work. I mixed freely with all groups and did not even think about cultural identity. I quickly made many friends from other backgrounds — German, Polish, Czech. We became good beer-drinking friends who freely joked about each other's ethnic background and visited one another's homes. I was invited to join the "Barons" — a fraternity of young men from all kinds of backgrounds. I easily made lasting friendships with many of them. My sister's wedding at my home parish of Christ the King featured one of the most ethnically mixed choirs ever, as all my friends joined together to sing at her wedding. The only thing that was strange was that when I studied psychology or sociology, it always seemed that we were studying about people who were totally different from me. I understood the subject matter and did well in it, but it never seemed to apply to me. It seemed like they were always speaking about someone else.

I had decided to study chemistry and social sciences because I was interested in working with people by becoming either a medical doctor or a psychiatrist. Yet as university studies proceeded I became more and more convinced that the best way to work with people — especially my own people, many of whom were poor, uneducated, and unemployed — would be through the church. The archbishop of San Antonio, Robert E. Lucey, was an untiring champion of the rights of the poor and of the need to work for a just society. He consistently brought to light the many injustices that condemned Mexicans and blacks to a life of perpetual poverty and misery. People disliked him because he stood up for the oppressed and marginated of society, because he dared to proclaim what others tried to hide and ignore.

I realized that I was one of the fortunate ones. God had given me the opportunity for a good education. Yet the masses of my people did not have such opportunities. I started to struggle with the sense of an obligation to dedicate my life to the betterment of my people. More and more, I found myself dropping by chapel to be alone with God to discern what I should do with myself. I never spoke to anyone about this except God, and the final decision was between God and myself. By the time I started to seek information on how to become a priest, I already knew that I would be one. From then on, there were never any doubts in my mind. I have now been ordained twenty-three years and still have no doubts or regrets about that core decision of my life made over thirty years ago in the chapel of St. Mary's University.

I went to the seminary with very high expectations, which were very soon shattered. Not only was the level of teaching quite mediocre, but in many ways it was evident that Mexicans were not welcome. The few Mexicans who entered the seminary were consistently subjected to endurance tests of one sort or another. Some transferred to other seminaries, others dropped out all together, a few others went on to become Protestant ministers. A minimal number like myself managed to survive — probably because we saw the seminary more as an obstacle course to be conquered than a place for learning and development.

In the seminary we were immediately classified as Mexicans and therefore slow learners — incapable of making good grades. Even symbolically, this idea was strengthened by the fact that Mexican sisters cooked and did the priests' laundry while the Anglo priests taught the classes. There were always racial slurs and lots of laughter and ridicule about the stupid practices of Mexican Catholics. I hated it! Seminary for me was a bad experience.

Many Mexican-Americans were chased out of the seminary for one stupid reason or another. If there are not many Mexican-American Catholic priests in the United States, it is precisely because the church did not want us. The faculty made it very difficult for the Hispanic seminarians and in one way or another, many were forced to quit. I was never as conscious of my "Mexican deficiencies" as I was while going through seminary. Many years later, when I started to meet other Mexican-American priests from different parts of the country, I learned that they had all had similar experiences.

The professors were not bad men. They were excellent. They were simply suffering from cultural myopia. Anything that did not conform to their U.S. Catholicism was wrong and stupid. And that is the way it was in all seminaries and religious communities. They were simply products of the racist society and the pre–Vatican II, Irish-German religious culture of their time. They were seminary professors and might know many things, but they were uninformed and wrong. The time would come when things would change and they themselves would be all the richer for it.

Why did I stay in the seminary? There were many reasons. The seminary experience was not totally negative — just the classes and formation program. I developed many good friends both among the faculty and the seminarians. Summers were good and we often visited one another. I started to become close friends with seminarians of German, Polish, and Czech background and would visit them in their ethnic communities. Some of the best times I have ever had were with them. By their bringing me into their families and by my inviting them to become part of my family we were becoming a new family — our differences were no longer barriers to our friendship. Quite the opposite, they were sources of fun and enrichment.

But even the good times with the seminarians would not have been enough had it not been for the constant support of the Carmelite priests of my home parish. I visited them often and they were always most hospitable, friendly, and encouraging. The pastor, Father Gus, virtually ordained me and let me take a very active part in all the liturgical celebrations of the parish. They always told me not to take the seminary seriously, that it was simply a necessary evil — like purgatory!

Old Father Felix, who perpetually puffed on a Dutch cigar, would always say: "Just hurry up and get it over with, boy." Their advice worked.

Neither/Nor but Something New

What helped me the most during these difficult years of much confusion were the summers at home. I continued to work in the grocery store and to visit with all my neighborhood friends. There we joked, complained, argued; there we lived and celebrated life. It was in the store that in totally undefined ways the riddle of life in San Antonio became clarified. It was there that new life was emerging... the life of the Mexican-American *mestizaje*.

Between the school years at the seminary and the summers at the store, I gradually became more and more aware of the many things that I was not: I was not and would never be, even if I wanted to, a regular U.S.-American. Yet neither would I be a *puro mexicano*. There were identities that I knew that I was and was not at the same time: U.S.-American, Mexican, Spanish, Indian. Yet I was! My very being was a combination. I was a rich mixture but I was not mixed-up! In fact, I was more and more clear that my own inner identity was new and exciting. I started to enjoy the feeling of who I was: I was *not just* U.S.-American and *not just* Mexican but fully both and exclusively neither. I knew both perfectly even if I remained a mystery to them. And I was threatening to them since they knew I knew them, but they did not know me fully. I lived in two worlds, and the two worlds lived in me. That was wealth.

At the same time, we had not yet pronounced a word that could name who we were. We were an emerging people whose identity had not yet been named. Of the new identity — neither this nor that but fully both — there was no doubt whatsoever. Yet the search for a name would dominate the quest of artists, intellectuals, social scientists, and poets for decades to come. And as of today we have not yet succeeded in finding the proper family name for this new human group on the planet earth.

Chapter 3

A Violated People

The Masks of Suffering

To much of the Anglo-American community of the U.S., the Mexican-Americans appear as happy-go-lucky people who are easy to please and who have no greater goal in life than to have large families, plenty of flowers, and lots of fiestas. They are poor and simple because they are an inferior people who love to be close to the earth and spend most of their time playing guitars, singing, dancing, eating, joking, and taking siestas.

The Mexican-Americans, according to the accepted stereotypes created by Anglo-American society, do not advance because they prefer the simple things in life, to work with their hands rather than with their minds. They make good plumbers, carpenters, janitors, maids, printers, mechanics. Why, say the educators, burden them with higher education? Why bore them with academic courses? Why put them through useless exercises in algebra, geometry, and the hard sciences? They so love the Mexican-Americans that they want to keep them poor and simple.

Mexican help is good to have around because Mexicans are always happy and docile. They never give any problems to the Anglo-Saxon masters. They have a quick smile as they respond with a polite, "Yes, Sir," or "Yes, Ma'am," as if it were a great privilege to be in the presence of their Anglo lords. They appear to be satisfied with so little.

The religious practices of the people appear simple and to many they appear superstitious. Regular mass attendance on Sundays is not ordinary for the majority of the people, but on holidays and special occasions, a visit to the Mexican Catholic church is a must. A visit to the *Virgen de Guadalupe,* an occasional pilgrimage to the sanctuary of *Nuestra Señora de los Lagos,* a stop to light a candle, a baptism or a mass for one of the *difuntos* of the family are the religious practices they take seriously. The majority of the people do not appear to be concerned with the doctrinal complexities of the church and seem quite content with a little *agua bendita* (holy water) and with the *altarcitos* (small altars) in the homes. Even the officials of the church are content with this simple church life since they can send the elderly or sickly priests to minister to the "simple needs of the Mexicans."

Yet behind the many masks of tranquility and docility lie the pent-up anger and frustration of generations of oppression, rape, robbery, insult, murder, and exploitation. That anger and frustration were latent for many years, but during the years prior to World War II, the growing numbers of Mexican-Americans and their increasing frustrations produced a volcano ready to erupt, and erupt it certainly would.

When you have no other choice in life than to accept the situation or die, you accept. You learn to put up with things not because you like them or approve of them, not because you are not willing to fight to bring about change, but because you realize that in the here and now, acceptance and passive resistance are the only ways to survive the present. You enable other generations to be born so that in time they might bring about the necessary changes demanded by the deepest yearnings of the human heart.

I can well remember one of my early assignments as a

priest while Lyndon B. Johnson was president. The whole country was excited about initiating programs that would eliminate poverty. It was a fantastic dream. I was stationed in a small country parish and tried to establish a youth program that would pay minimum wages while the youth were in training for future jobs. When the program was about to start, some of the Mexican-American leadership of the town came to speak with me. To my great amazement, they asked me to drop the program.

I could not believe what I was hearing. Crazy thoughts went quickly through my mind: Were they jealous that their children were going to get a good wage? Didn't they trust me? Didn't they want their children to get ahead? Maybe they just liked being poor and didn't want to change!

Then they started to explain. The Mexican-Americans in that area worked for about one-third the minimum wage. Yet the whole area was controlled by the large landowners. As long as the people did not make trouble, they were safe to enjoy their simple life. But if they started to work for any change in the status quo, one or two members of the Mexican-American community would simply disappear. They loved the program I wanted to bring into the area, but they did not want to disturb the status quo at the cost of their children's disappearance. So for the time being we dropped the program. There are many ways of keeping a people down and the fear of losing a loved one is one of the most effective.

It is true that sometimes people accept situations because they are afraid of risks or too lazy to take the initiative. Yet it is equally true that in certain circumstances the wise and prudent natural leaders of the people know from experience that the only option open for them to survive and to prepare for the ultimate liberation of the people is to accept the situation as it is and make the best of it. To accept it does not mean we like it or enjoy it; it is simply a way of coping with it in order to survive.

The Eruption

Given the growing numbers of people and the increasing anger and frustration, the eruption had to take place one way or another. But it was the experience of World War II that started the eruption, the massive exodus from slavery into freedom, not an exodus from one country to another, but an exodus from one state of life to another.

Before the war there had been various efforts for betterment. Some had been built around the need to form beneficial societies to bury our dead. Others had been built around patriotic feasts, and still others around religious celebrations — like the Guadalupanas. Civic organizations had started to help our young people become good Americans. We were in the U.S. to stay and the more quickly we forgot Spanish and became like everyone else, the better off we would be.

During World War II, for the first time in our collective experience in the U.S., our young men were being told in the same way as every other young man in the country, *"Uncle Sam Needs You!"* To be needed by the U.S.A.! From being marginated and exploited, to being needed by everybody else — an incredible experience of recognition, acceptance, and belonging. Our families proudly exhibited pictures of uniformed sons in the military and with great pride displayed the American flag on U.S. patriotic holidays. The U.S.A. had not always been kind to us, but it was our land and our country. It might not have loved us, but we loved it and loved it so much we were willing to give our lives for it. Our young men never resisted the draft or tried to claim exemptions. They did not even wait to be called. They quickly volunteered and went to the aid of their country.

In the military service, those who society had said were inferior and slow learners were quickly educated in the sophisticated art and science of modern warfare. They were taught to organize and to lead. They were motivated by talks about our civic obligation to defend the basic freedoms of humanity: liberty, justice, and equality. Tyranny had to be fought and destroyed. That was what the U.S. military and the American way of life were all about. And the chaplains preached the word of God: that there was no greater virtue than to die in the defense of the rights of life. God did not want us to be passive; God wanted us to fight for what was right. We were equipped with knowledge and techniques, motivated civilly and strengthened religiously. What more could we want?

In Europe and in Asia, our men had new experiences of equality. They could eat and drink in the same restaurants, date the same girls, wear the same clothes, and all be identified as Yankees. We were equal in battle and equal in fun. In the war, there was no question about our national identity and allegiance. Many of our men were awarded the Congressional Medal of Honor. Yet, when the bodies of our young men who had been willing to be sacrificed for the sake of freedom and equality were returned home, many of them were not allowed to be buried in their home cemeteries because they were Mexicans. In the good old Texas tradition, Anglos and Mexicans could never mix — even in the cemeteries. Good enough to die for the country abroad, but not good enough to be buried in the home ground with fellow Americans.

It was the returning veterans who first sounded the trumpet call of the new battle that was to be fought at home. *Ya basta!* (Enough is enough!) became the slogan of the new movements of the nonmilitary, yet very militant, wars waged against institutionalized poverty, segregation, legitimated exploitation, and sacralized racism. All the gods had to be stripped naked so that the truth might appear. If we had fought against imperialistic and racist tyranny abroad, it was now our moral obligation before God and society to fight against it at home. If we had defeated the genetically pure "Master Race" in Germany and in Japan, now we had to defeat the "Master Race" concept within our own U.S.A. so that authentic Americanism — freedom and justice for all and the right to the pursuit of happiness — could truly be enjoyed by all the citizens of the land and not just the WASPish whites. Our people now had the know-how and the civic and religious motivation. Generations of frustration and come to an end. The time for a new beginning had arrived. The volcano erupted!

The Eruption Continues

Soon after I was ordained in 1963 and started to get involved as a priest in the life around San Antonio, I quickly discovered that I was one of a privileged minority within an underprivileged minority group. My past experience, though many times difficult and painful, had generally speaking been positive in comparison to the multiple negative experiences of the majority of my people. I was not rich, materially speaking, but I was certainly privileged and well-off when it came to the many beautiful and positive experiences of my years of growing up. Yet that was all the more reason why I could not ignore the painful situation of the majority of my people.

The 1960s were times of great agitation and profound questioning. The hidden anger of a sleepy and festive people was erupting violently all over the United States. The *campesinos* in California were rising against the powerful landowners under the prophetic leadership of César Chávez. In the U.S.A., a country that prides itself in proclaiming liberty and justice for all, all legislation that protects workers has consistently excluded farmworkers. Not only have they been excluded from the protection of the law, but workers have been brought in from Mexico — even when we had large numbers of Mexican-Americans unemployed — to harvest the crops at salaries much lower than those paid to the already underpaid Mexican-American farmworkers. Slavery was officially eliminated in the U.S., but farmworkers have continued to be treated worse than slaves: no protection of the law, living conditions often unfit for animals, no sanitary facilities in the fields, no medical care, no protection from powerful insecticides used to fumigate the corps, harsh working conditions under the blistering sun. These people are forced to work under conditions you would expect in some right-wing dictatorship or in a concentration camp, but not in the U.S.A.

But the *campesinos* were not the only ones who were beginning to speak out. The landless *mexicano españoles* of New Mexico, who had previously been happy to see their daughters marry wealthy Anglo landowners, were now reclaiming the titles to many of the rich lands in New Mexico. New Mexico had been the most populated and best civilized frontier of Mexico at the beginning of the great Yankee invasion. Yet with the U.S. takeover, Anglo laws were imposed and the old land titles that had been in effect were disregarded. Many of the New Mexicans were robbed of their lands through legal trickery of the new government. Yet these people, who belonged to the land that had belonged to them for generations, would not easily forget. The time had arrived to settle the many accounts of the injustices of the past.

A new political party, *La Raza Unida,* was organizing and taking power in the rural areas of Texas where all power had been the unquestioned property of the Anglo landed aristocracy. For the first time, the traditional political parties were being challenged. Previously the Democratic party had taken Mexican-Americans for granted and, after obtaining their vote, ignored them. Now the people were forming their own political party, and in many of the rural areas, they started to win all the elections.

But such far-reaching movements were only the first tremors of the eruption. Students started to organize and speak up in the schools and universities. The unquestioned authority of the gods of the educational system was not only being questioned but seriously challenged by the voices of those who had been condemned to silent inferiority. It was not the Mexican-American students who had not made passing grades, but the school system itself that had failed the people. Society had ingeniously created and perpetuated mediocrity to legitimate its own racist attitudes and convictions. But now it was being exposed, and the so-called scientific evidence concerning the biological and psychological inferiority of minorities was easily demolished — although it would not easily disappear.

Once the blaze of protest ignited, it spread like a wild forest fire. People started to question and expose discrimination in their jobs, in the public media of communications, in the courts of law, in jury selection, in business, in the military, in banking-loan practices, in real estate sales, in country club membership. Discrimination was everywhere and showed itself in many more ways than anyone had even suspected. No institution of society was left unchallenged.

The blaze soon reached religion and the churches. They had not only been guilty of standing by silently while the massive rape of their people had been taking place, but in many ways they had contributed to it — maybe not maliciously, but nevertheless really. In some ways the church had been the champion of the poor and the voice of the voiceless. For instance, Archbishop Robert E. Lucey of San Antonio was an early pioneer of desegregation and social rights. From his arrival in San Antonio in the 1940s until his death in 1977, he was a fearless and tireless prophet who denounced the contradictions of systems that kept people down and refused to allow their God-given talents to flourish and develop. He developed many enemies, even among his fellow bishops, clergymen, and flock, because of his defense of the poor and the defenseless. He was great, but he was a rare exception.

The church was anti-Mexican-American in many of its

attitudes. People were driven out of the church. As some pastors clearly stated, "You did not pay for this church. It is not yours. Get out." Others were ignored, insulted, or ridiculed. Seminarians were driven out of the seminaries and many of the religious orders of men had an overabundance of Mexican-American lay brothers to do the domestic work; hardly any of them were allowed into the priesthood. The religious orders acted as if the Mexican-American's vocation were to remain silent and submissive in the humble service of the Anglo priests. The Mexican-American women religious were often sent to do the laundry and kitchen work but were seldom allowed to function as teaching sisters.

Mexican-American laity, sisters, and priests began to organize groups to protest discrimination within the church itself. The urgency of the moment and the needs of our people did not permit us to remain silent. We had to speak and challenge even at the risk of being chastised and condemned. One seminarian, Albert Benavides, who later went on to become an outstanding priest, was denied ordination simply because he attended a meeting of concerned Hispanic priests. For this, he was labeled subversive, dangerous, and not sufficiently mature. The bishops, church educators, and pastors were blind. They could not understand the protest and cries of indignation of a people who wanted to be faithful Catholics, but were not allowed to be so by the very leadership of the church.

The church was not being confronted by those who wanted to leave, but by those who wanted to belong. It did not know what was happening when groups such as PADRES or LAS HERMANAS protested the lack of Hispanic priests or nuns, the discrimination in the seminaries and convents, the lack of Spanish in the liturgy, the scandalous lack of Hispanic bishops. The U.S. Catholic church was over 25 percent Hispanic and there were over 200 bishops, but there was not a single Hispanic bishop in the U.S. Of 50,000 Catholic priests, not even 200 were native-born Hispanics.

Some of the extreme militant groups were blaming the church for the generations of racist oppression. They said that the church had been like a mother who silently and permissively stood by watching while her boyfriends consistently raped her daughter. It was not a pretty image, but in many ways it had been (and sadly enough still continues to be) very true. Some had tried becoming Protestant, but there too they had met the same attitudes. So the answer: reject all religion. Religion had sacralized racism and thus had been its ultimate legitimization. To them it seemed that the only way to help Mexican-Americans gain their basic human dignity was to kill all religion so that the ultimate root of racism might be destroyed forever.

At protest meetings I was told in no uncertain terms, "If you want to be of help, get out of the way. Your church only kept us down by preaching obedience to the *gringo* masters. How do you want to control us now?" It was not easy to take but there was much truth in what they were saying. The serious accusations forced me and many others to take a much deeper and more critical look at the inner functioning of our church and, even deeper yet, of religion itself. How does religion function in relation to the dominant society, in relation to an oppressed people? For the first time I started to realize that religion, even my own Christian-Catholic religion, could function as a powerful tool of oppression. I was frightened! So many of the things we had dared to say and do "In God's name" all of a sudden appeared scandalous. I started to ask deeper questions about my church, my religion, and about the gospel itself.

Going to the Roots

As we started to struggle for freedom and equality within society, we also started to ask deeper questions about ourselves, about our families, about our heritage, about our past. It was not sufficient to become a professional or to get rich. We needed much more. We had been marginated not just because we were poor but because we were Mexican. But we were not Mexican citizens. We were fully U.S.-Americans, just as much as anyone else. Yet there was something definitely distinct about us. Just who were we? Where did we come from? Why were we the way we were?

We needed answers, not to apologize to anyone for who we were, but to know ourselves. Our schools had never taught us about ourselves: our literature, our history, our customs, our traditions, our foods. We had studied about everyone else but never about ourselves. Our story had been either totally absent or completely misrepresented by the history books of the schools, universities, and seminaries. Latin American church history was totally missing from the learned tomes of church history, as if it didn't even exist, even though 50 percent of the entire Catholic church is in Latin America.

All of a sudden we had discovered a fascinating new entity — ourselves. Before, we had lived our identity in silence and solitude, almost as if we were not supposed to be. We had sheepishly apologized, joked, ignored. But now we could be. We could study ourselves and our origins. We could openly celebrate our traditions and speak about ourselves from within our own experience. We discovered that in order to truly affirm ourselves, we had to be able to retell our story — the story of the great pilgrimage of our ancestors that had led us to be who we are today. So we started to go seriously into our past, and what a fascinating and liberating revelation it would prove to be. History is not merely the record of the past but the life-source of the present and the hidden energy for the new future.

As a people, we had been born as a result of the U.S. invasion and subsequent conquest of the great northern regions of Mexico from California to Texas. And before that our Mexican ancestors had been born out of the invasion and conquest of pre-Columbian Mexico. As the Spanish conquest of Mexico had tried to suppress everything native, so the Anglo conquest of northern Mexico had tried to suppress and destroy everything Mexican. We could say that in recent historical times, we had been twice conquered, twice victimized, and twice mesticized. Through each conquest, the native soil with its culture and inhabitants had been deeply penetrated but not destroyed. The conquerors had tried to destroy the natives, but in time they would be absorbed and conquered by the product of their own unsuspected creation. Like the womb of a woman receiving the seed of a man to produce new life, so in Mexico and subsequently in the Southwest of today's U.S., a new child had been conceived and born.

We needed to know our parents in order to know who we were. We knew the U.S.-American side. In the classrooms and in the movies, we had learned well about the great experiment in democracy, about the Boston Tea Party and the rebellion against taxation without representation, about the American war of independence in 1776, about the constitutional convention, and about the birth of the great republic of the United States of America. Its historical development had been as fascinating as it had been ambiguous. We had learned about the greatness of the American experience and we held it in great reverence. What we had not studied was the cruel injustices involved in the process of nation building: the massacres of the natives, the slave trade, the systematic impoverishment of the Mexican inhabitants of the Southwest.

So now we started to discover the treasures of ancient Mexico. Our school books had always spoken about the Indians as backward savages. What an illuminating discovery to find that our ancient Mexican ancestors from New Mexico to the valley of Anahuac were highly sophisticated and civilized peoples whose scientific achievements were in many ways far ahead of European civilization: medicine, art, philosophy, architecture, commerce, education, astronomy, agriculture. Many of our common foods today are of native origins: chocolate, tomatoes, potatoes, chile beans, corn, turkeys. The ways of life were humanizing: proper upbringing of the young people, respect for the elders and their ways, respect for the dignity of the other.

It is true that Christian Europe was much more advanced in one important area: warfare. Europeans had developed the physical power to impose their ways upon everyone else and, sadly enough, in a time accustomed to sacred wars, it was considered ordinary to justify war and conquest for the sake of the gospel. Europe had conquered and destroyed, and it attempted through the power of the written word to justify its actions. With its weapons it subjected natives' bodies, and with its knowledge, philosophy, and religion it tried to dominate natives' souls. Or rather, it tried to annihilate them.

In spite of the negative aspects of the European conquest, we cannot deny our Iberian ancestry. Like it or not, Spain is part of our heritage. In the U.S. we had been subjected to the famous "Black Legend," which clearly detailed all the crimes of the Spanish conquest. Based on the writings of Bartolomé de las Casas, who had staunchly defended the Indians of Mexico against the abuses of the Spaniards, the English and the French set out to discredit Spain. They wrote about the Spanish conquest of Latin America as if the devil himself had masterminded it. The Spanish conquest was contrasted to the English conquest of native America, which was presented as a pure and undefiled act of divine providence. Everything Spain had done was presented as evil, while everything England had done was presented as divine. The Black Legend never had anything good to say about Spain, so we grew up with the image that every Spaniard was a perverse and corrupt lover of violence, gold, and wealth obtained through the exploitation of others.

Once again we were in for a fascinating discovery as we

started to find our Iberian roots. Spain of 1492 was the product of a long struggle for freedom. After centuries of inva-
sions — from the Romans to the Moslems, who finally left
Spain in January of 1492 — Spain had to struggle against its
invaders to maintain its identity and eventually its independence. Yet each invasion had brought in something new that
blended with the Iberian ways, giving the Spanish way of life
an ever richer texture.

Under very harsh conditions, Spaniards had maintained
their drive for dignity, identity, and liberty. Hundreds of years
of captivity had never dampened their spirit and their quest
for life. Maybe this long experience is at the core of the Spanish soul, which seems to thrive amid tensions and contradictions: in the bullfight, tiny man triumphs over the majestic
and powerful beast.

During this time of struggle, Spain had developed beautiful literature, music, and dance. The profound religious
commitment of the people — with its *virgenes* and penitential
processions that fill the streets with long lighted candles carried by silent, hooded persons — is a reflection of the eternal
rhythms of the human struggle. Philosophy, with it multiple
distinctions about unending questions, and law, with its in-
tricate precisions in the defense of the rights of persons and
of nations, were flourishing in Spain as was the new quest for
biblical knowledge, a quest to return to the originating roots
of the Christian tradition. Out of the struggle had come new
life. Suffering had not killed the Spanish soul. Quite the contrary. Through its indomitable will to live, it had not only
survived, not only preserved that which was native to the
soil itself, but had created and produced the flourishing of
new life that is Spain today.

If in the invasion of Mexico there had been cruelty, there
had also been heroic goodness. History is always ambiguous. The missioners had been the valiant defenders of the
Indians, at least at the beginning of the conquest. Bartolomé

de las Casas crossed the Atlantic thirteen times to demand justice and protection for the Indians. Vasco de Quiroga organized gospel villages wherein a truly evangelical civilization could thrive. The missionaries tried to evangelize the Indians while preserving many of their native ways. They sought to protect them from the abuses of the *conquistadores,* even to the point of being killed themselves for being troublemakers to the crown. The religious expressions of the common folk of Spain easily blended with the religious expressions of the natives of Mexico, thus forming a new religion that would find its complete fusion in the Virgin of Guadalupe.

Being descendants of Spaniards was no shame. As we came to know, appreciate, and make our own the mystically dynamic tradition and heritage of Spain, we could hold our heads up with great pride to be descendants of these noble pioneers of the development of the human spirit, of the protection and purification of our Catholic faith, and of the great codes of international law.

Being the children of Iberians and natives and discovering ourselves to be neither conqueror nor conquered, but the children of both, gave complete new meaning and direction to our present situation. We no longer had to reject our past; we could now assume it and transcend it as a child assumes and transcends the heritage received from both parents. We no longer had to say, "I am not a Spaniard," or, "I am not an Indian," for we could now say with great pride, "I am Mexican."

Yet just as the young Mexican nation was beginning to take its first baby steps into nationhood, it was invaded, conquered, and violated by the bully next door. In the 1830s the massive legal and illegal migrations from the North started into the frontiers of Mexican territory. Those from the North came with nothing but disdain. They considered Indians and blacks inferior, the Spanish Catholics perverted, and the mix-

breeds of Spanish and Indian horrible mongrels who had in-
herited the worst of two bad races.

The United States was founded with a spirit of secular
mission. The founding fathers brought with them from England the conviction that they were God's chosen people for
the domination of the world. The British had considered
themselves to be the true Israel, since, in their opinion, God
had rejected the historical Israel in favor of the people who
lived in the Isles. The British immigrants who crossed the sea
to the new land of opportunity would apply the same logic
and see themselves as the new Israel. It was, as perceived by
them, their sacred obligation to establish the new world order
and to spread it to the ends of the earth.

The great British expansion moved urgently with a sense
of unquestioned sacred obligation. This would become the
Manifest Destiny of the new nation that was to take its way
of life to the very tip of Argentina. Thus it was not surprising that shortly after the new nation won its independence,
it would start to move West to take over the rest of the vast
lands we call the Americas. The new experiment in human
government was one of the great breakthroughs in human
history, yet it was very limited, for it benefited the "new chosen people" and not the others. The rest of the world would
participate by being subject to the new masters. The settlers
saw themselves as freedom fighters and liberators; others saw
them as invaders and oppressors.

The generations of abuse, brutality, and violence made
many Mexican-Americans hate everything *gringo*. Everything Mexican appeared as heavenly and everything *gringo*
appeared as diabolical. The many atrocities that we had suffered in the multiple holocaust-like situations could now be
spoken about and denounced. The United States was not
used to hearing such denunciations about itself. The new
prophets were quickly labelled anti-American and Marxists.
If the "Mexicans" did not like it here, let them go back home.

They forgot that this was our home and that we had always been here. Accusations about American abuses rattled puritanical and lily-white minds.

As many Anglos objected and denounced the accusers, many others listened and joined the struggle for justice and liberty. New partnerships were formed and we started to rediscover the U.S. and Americanism with a new objectivity and a new pride. It was not the system itself that was wrong, but the way the system functioned in relation to the various non-Anglo groups of this country. It was our task, our newly discovered "Manifest Destiny," to help forge a new America ever more loyal to the principles upon which it was founded.

It is not a question of hating anyone or any tradition, but appreciating each one in its uniqueness and its limitations. It is not a question of rejection but of the radical acceptance of the totality of our concrete and historical being. It is a question of being able to affirm without doubt, question, or hesitation: "I am."

It has taken a long time to discover our parentage, and we still have a long way to go, but we are beginning to discover with pride, to formulate with precision, and to proclaim with joy the presence of our identity — our new *mestizaje*. It is no longer a time of shame or denial, but one of assuming, claiming as our own, and transcending. It is the springtime of the new human creation.

Chapter 4

Marginality

In the last twenty years, great strides have been made toward the eradication of racism, classism, and the various types of social injustice that dominate the scene of socio-economic life in the Southwest. New alliances and friendships have pierced through previously impenetrable barriers and have opened new doors of understanding and cooperation. But we have an even longer way to travel over roads that have not yet been designed. Racism, ethnocentrism, and classism are very deeply ingrained in the fibers that make up the culture of the U.S.A. They will not easily disappear, but serious beginnings are indeed being made.

Even though the "No Mexicans Allowed" signs are gone, there is no doubt that there are still many real and very obvious markers that enforce the same exclusion. It is still much easier to cross the legal boundary between Mexico and the United States than to cross through many of the long-established and deeply-entrenched socio-cultural borders that very effectively maintain a segregated existence. It is far easier to pass laws of desegregation than to create a desegregated culture. And today, the culture of segregation still reigns throughout the Americas: in the United States, in Latin America, and in my own city of San Antonio.

Festive Breakthrough

As a child, as a young college student, and even now as a middle-aged priest, I have always looked forward to the great Fiesta of San Antonio. I love the parades, the carnivals, the cotton-candy, the crazy rides, and the street-dancing. I love to mingle with people from all walks of life, of all ages and all colors, who at the moment of the Fiesta have one thing in common: the celebration of life. There is a profound experience of communion and commonality among the people celebrating Fiesta.

Yet I suspect that there is no time and no place where the social barriers are more visibly displayed than during the annual Fiesta Week, when people from throughout the city — which is predominantly Mexican-American — join together to celebrate the final victory of the Texas forces over the Mexican troops headed by General Santa Anna. It is an ironic and curious celebration. It is presided over by King Antonio, who is always an Anglo from an exclusively Anglo association known as the Texas Cavaliers. The King of the Fiesta rushes throughout the city visiting schools, which in some areas are 100 percent Mexican-American, receiving the enthusiastic acclaims of all his subjects. He is a living symbol for the schoolchildren that the white man still is supreme. This racial pageantry got so bad that the king has been prohibited from visiting some of the predominantly Mexican-American schools.

Today out of the ranks of a Mexican-American organization called LULAC (League of United Latin American Citizens), a Rey Feo — ugly king — is beginning to outdo King Antonio and co-presides with him over the festivities of San Antonio. In the very midst of Fiesta and in a merry way in the royal courts of make-believe, the struggle for desegregation is taking place in profound ways that will probably have more long-term effects than many laws. Symbolic of the new existence, anyone can and has been Rey Feo: Mexican-American, Anglo, Jew.

During the main parade of the week, the Battle of Flowers, the duchesses and queens, who are always Anglos and never Mexican-American, proudly parade through the streets of the city playing the part of ancient royalty, which they never were. I suppose it is their own brand of fairy-tale: the land robbers of the past install themselves and their progeny as the nobility of their new acquisitions. Their robes and crowns easily mask the multiple injustices of the past. They majestically and silently preside over the thousands of spectators who enjoy the parade as if they were watching a museum of past artifacts marching through the streets of San Antonio. The beautiful dresses are admired, but the persons wearing them are hardly noticed and soon forgotten. Plastic mannequins would play the role just as well and not many would notice the difference. I doubt if anyone except their close friends and relatives even know their names. My mother used to take us to the parade to admire the beautiful dresses, but there was never a word said about those wearing the dresses; to this day I have never noticed the name of any of the reigning royalty of the Fiesta.

The garden parties of the Alamo and the coronation of the king and queen remain the exclusive domain of the descendants of the *norteamericano* immigrants, many who came illegally and decided to rebel against their host country. Yet in order to raise money to carry out these exclusive extravaganzas, their own members operate a "Night in Old San Antonio," at which Mexican food, along with the other ethnic foods of San Antonio, is enjoyed by all without exception. Festivities for all San Antonians abound throughout the city and there segregation is nowhere in sight. The people freely mingle, enjoy one another's presence, and celebrate the new creation that is taking shape all around us and within our very selves in San Antonio.

During the new Saturday night parade, which is all lit up with lights and flares — almost like a civic Easter Vigil with the new light of the Easter candle — it is Miss San Antonio who presides to the massive acclaim of the people. She is chosen from among the college students of San Antonio and *anyone* is eligible to be Miss San Antonio. Throughout the year, it is she, not the queen, who represents San Antonians throughout the country and abroad.

As the colorful and festive student bands and marching units, often composed entirely of Mexican-Americans, parade past the great stone monument to the heroes of the Alamo, the contrast is clear: the conquerors of the past live on in stone monuments while the children of the conquered walk joyfully and with great pride down the streets of their own city. Fiesta is a special celebration of desegregating San Antonio, of the old factions that want to maintain the old order and of the new generations that are transcending it and creating a new one. Friendships, alliances, and marriages that break through the old taboos are being formed and new life is emerging everywhere. It is not easy. There is frequently pain, but it is the joyful pain of childbirth, of the new society being born.

Fiesta is the mysterious and mystical celebration of a battle that was won long ago and of a new *mestizaje* that is today taking over. Out of the remains of the victorious and of the defeated of yesterday, new life is emerging today. Like the great phoenix of ancient mythology, it cannot be stopped. Fiesta is not the celebration of victory or defeat, but of the new life of the land. This life has not been defined, but it is being experienced in the rich ethnic mix of the dances, food, music, parades, and rituals that are the great Fiesta of San Antonio.

Institutional Barriers

The old social barriers, still so evident during Fiesta week, are experienced frequently in daily life. A few years ago, at the request of the Pentagon, I visited U.S. bases throughout West Germany to explore racial injustices within the military system. Nowhere were they so obvious as along the West Germany-East Germany border. There, where the young men and women had nothing to do but patrol borders, the very high percentage of brown and black faces was quickly evident. The further away you got from the front and into the more exciting technological and electronic jobs, the more you saw white faces. And in the higher ranks? There was a token presence of Hispanics and blacks but not nearly enough in relation to the very high percentage of Hispanics and blacks in the lower ranks.

Recently a man in my parish told me his experience. He saw a job notice for a computer operator for a government job at Kelly Field in San Antonio. He is a very dark-skinned, small man who tends to be rather shy. When he went to see about the job, he was immediately told by one of the Anglo secretaries that there had been no janitorial openings announced and that he must be mistaken. When he inquired specifically about the computer job, she answered with great surprise: "Oh, you're looking for *that* job." Her presupposition had been that he was qualified only for janitorial work.

With the increasing phobia in the United States that tries to keep out Mexican and Latin American nationals, U.S. citizens of Hispanic background are experiencing a new, semi-legalized segregation. Because the employers are being threatened with sanctions for hiring foreigners who have entered the country illegally, many simply refuse to hire any dark-skinned person who "looks Mexican." Blacks and whites, on the other hand, can move around easily without any need to establish their citizenship.

Recently in San Antonio a mentally retarded adult who was under heavy medication wandered out into the street by himself. He was caught by the immigration services. Presumed to be a Mexican because he would not speak English (he would not speak at all), he was deported to Mexico. It took several days before his parents were able to trace him in Mexico and bring him back to his legitimate home in the United States.

The distances are evident in clubs and restaurants: the majority of the waiters, busboys, and clean-up personnel are dark skinned. But it is equally present in banks. You might find a Hispanic vice-president to deal with the lucrative Latin American trade, but generally no dark-skinned persons are in areas of high responsibility. At a recent graduation of the University of Texas at San Antonio there were very few Mexican-American graduates in sight. They were present, but few in numbers in comparison to their high visibility throughout the city. The news media have Hispanics working in menial jobs, but none in positions of visibility or responsibility.

Today, Hispanic youth are dropping out of high school faster than ever. Poverty forces many to stay away from school because of the lack of proper clothing. Often they have to start work quite young in order to help with the support of the family. We have fewer Hispanics in higher education today than we had ten years ago. The escalating cost of higher education is making it possible only to the wealthy and will increasingly keep the poor out of the institutions of higher learning. The walls between the "haves" and the "have-nots" are once again being built and the gap that separates them will grow larger and larger — at least for the time being, at least until new movements for justice and equality begin to take force.

A friend of mine once said that the only institution in which we are well represented is jails. Even though it is an established fact that just as much crime takes place among Anglos, it is the Hispanics and blacks who end up in the jails. Many come from poor backgrounds and cannot afford the expensive lawyers that are demanded by our justice system, a system quick and merciful for those who can afford it but slow and demanding for those who cannot.

The churches have not been exempted from the racism. Hispanics find it difficult to enter seminaries, and even when they manage to enter, misunderstanding on the part of the seminary professors and directors forces most of them out. I attended a White House conference of Hispanic educators a few years ago. The outstanding participants had doctoral degrees and were well-known for their publications. I was astonished to discover that two out of three educators with whom I visited were ex-seminarians. All of them had been dropped from the seminary because they "could not make the grade."

Many excellent men who want to be priests are still prevented from orders because of racism and ethnocentrism within the seminaries. Lip service is paid to "responding to the needs of the Hispanics" by those in positions of authority, but sometimes I feel that nothing has really changed. Hispanics will be accepted in U.S. Catholicism only to the degree that they cease to be Hispanic and conform to the way of Anglo-American institutions. In spite of all the talk of Hispanic ministry — in a church over 30 percent Hispanic — many Hispanics are still being driven out of the churches by pastoral agents who are not sensitive to their needs. A few Hispanic men have been named bishops, but as a whole their presence seems to have been lost in the assembly of bishops and in the total church.

All the institutions of our society have successfully kept the Hispanics at a safe distance. Some few have made it in, but it is an ongoing struggle. Hispanics still have to prove themselves much more than others. They cannot simply be "as good as" but they must be better even to qualify. The institutional barriers are the most difficult ones to crack, but cracks are being made.

Invisible Mechanisms

One does not have to look very far to discover the social barriers. The explanations of why they persist are multiple and complex. Their origins are deeply rooted in ancient times and past rivalries. Certain colors have always been associated with good and evil, superiority and inferiority, beauty and ugliness. From birth we are conditioned to see angelic beauty in the white, the blond, the blue-eyed. The liturgical colors sacralizes our color coding: white is pure and festive while black and brown are negative or non-existent. White baby Jesus and blonde Virgin Mary. We learn to fear darkness and to look upon it as evil.

We are conditioned to view lighter-skinned people as more intelligent, dignified, and developed. We rejoice with anticipation at certain color combinations and recoil with fear at others. Racism is not rational, but it is very real; it is spontaneous, but very profound; it is a human construction, but it appears most natural.

We find comfort in our own ways and fear the unknown, which often appears as a threat to our own existence. We must conquer and dominate it before it destroys us. We must create defense systems to protect our boundaries and our interests. Monuments are created to venerate with pride our way of life. Literature brings out the beauty of our language. Our religion assures us that we have the approval of the all-powerful Author of life itself. We carefully cultivate a way of life with its values, foods, music, sense of humor, and wisdom. It becomes our world and it appears as natural, as the way for humanity itself.

Yet within our own group, we need to experience success by getting ahead. Western civilization has created and sanctioned the culture of conquering heroes and superstars. You have to be number one in order to be humanly satisfied. Nothing else will do. Thus we struggle to get ahead of others, whether in business or in sports. We create institutions to increase and protect our gains. We operate impersonally through others and are even totally unaware of the masses of people that have to be exploited in order for us to get ahead. The beautiful people who can afford to eat the proper diet and attend the health clubs to burn off excess calories, the jet-set who are equally at home in Rio, Paris, or San Antonio, the credit-card holders who can get whatever they want, this super-class emerges as a transnational race.

The higher one is on the racial-ethnic class scale of importance and wealth, the more threatened one's very existence is by desegregation. When one's existence is defined and made possible by the structures of segregation, then the questioning of these structures questions life itself. Liberation for the segregated and oppressed will mean death for those who have enjoyed the fruits of a segregated existence — not personal death but death to the life they have been accustomed to.

The fear of the other who poses a threat to segregated society will trigger collective defense mechanisms so that society as it has been may continue to be. These reactions are due not to the evil intentions of any one person, but the collective psyche of a particular group that is determined to survive. This does not come as a result of meetings and deliberations. It is the spontaneous desire to live.

But even stronger is the oppressed's desire to live and to put an end to the dead existence they have been subjected to for many generations. Segregation is against nature. It is a sin against the Creator who made all of us together descendants of Adam and Eve. We are one human race, but sinful humanity insists on splitting us into segregating and fighting races — race against race, class against class, ethnic group against ethnic group. The strong prevail over the weak and proclaim their ways to be superior. The weak have no choice but to submit. But the inner drive toward wholeness cannot be extinguished. Human freedom seeks and struggles for the freedom and equality intended for us by the Creator.

Segregated peoples have no choice, if we are to be faithful to our Creator, than to struggle unceasingly for desegregation. We do not always know the way, but we have no doubt that ways must be found. Sometimes we grow tired, weary, and disillusioned, but we know that we must go on. Sometimes there is division among ourselves, but the demands of the movement are far more important than our personal differences. In our struggles we must find new ways, new models, new possibilities; otherwise we will just be forcing our way into the old segregated society and quickly find ourselves doing unto others what others previously did to us.

Real change is taking place. Efforts are being made, coalitions are being formed, and new leadership is emerging everywhere. The Mexican-American Southwest is being Anglocized at much the same pace that the Anglo Southwest of the U.S.A. is being Mexicanized. Neither group is simply allowing the other in; rather both are forming a new human space wherein all feel more at home. Some see it as scandalous while others see it as welcome, but regardless of how it is viewed, it is taking place. Culturally speaking, a new human group is in the making.

Chapter 5

My People Resurrect at Tepeyac

The Dawn of a New Day

Every year on the 12th of December, very early in the morning before the first rays of the sun break the darkness of the night, in continuity with our native ancestors who gathered each day to welcome the rising of the new sun and with early Christians who gathered early on Easter Sunday to welcome the first day of the new creation, Mexicans and Mexican-Americans gather in great numbers to dance the rituals of the ancient *matachines* and sing the *mañanitas* to the brown virgin of Guadalupe. We gather to welcome the new creation, the birth of our race, the *mestizo* people of the Americas.

Devotion to Our Lady of Guadalupe, the queen, empress, and mother of the Americas, expresses the deepest nationality of our people. I remember vividly and still look forward to celebrating today the great festivities surrounding the feast of Guadalupe: from the preparatory novenas, to the all-night dances of the *matachines,* to the pre-dawn massive gathering for the singing of the *mañanitas,* to the evening offering of flowers and crowning of our queen. She is not the museum-like queen of the San Antonio Fiesta, but the living queen-mother of life whose love and compassion continue to reign within our hearts. As I work on this manuscript,

children from throughout my parish are outside learning the
ritual dances from their parents. Each generation passes on
to the next the thread of life that binds us to our ancestors
and projects us into the future. The annual celebration of the
Guadalupe-event is not just a devotion or a large church gathering. It is the collective affirmation and cultic celebration of
life in spite of the multiple threats of death.

In Catholic elementary school they would tell us about
the *real* apparitions — Lourdes, Fatima. The apparition of
the Americas at Tepeyac was casually referred to as Mexican
folklore, an affair of the Indians, the religiosity of the uninformed. But in my home parish, Christ the King, the Virgin
of Guadalupe was celebrated in ways no other religious feast
in the Catholic calendar was celebrated. In those days I did
not know about the hierarchy of feasts in the official calendar
of the church, but in my own experience, there was no question that the main feast of the year was that of Our Lady of
Guadalupe.

Her presence was not only celebrated in the churches, but
she reigned maternally in all our homes, our places of business, our cars and buses, and even over the heads of the pilots
in modern-day jets. Her medal is worn over the hearts of millions of her children, and many young men going to war had
her image tattooed on their bodies to insure their protection.
Her banner has led and given courage to all the major efforts for liberation of the Mexican people — from the flag of
the war of independence of Father Hidalgo in 1810 to the
present-day struggles of César Chávez with the farmworkers
in California.

She not only appeared in the outskirts of Mexico City
in December of 1531, but she continues to appear today
throughout the Americas in the art, the poetry, the dra-
mas, the anthropological studies, the religious expressions,
the shrines, and the pilgrimages of her people. Rather than
saying that she appeared in 1531, it would be more accurate

to say that she started to appear — to be present among us —
in 1531 and that her visible, tangible, and motherly presence
continues to spread throughout the Americas.

Her story is not only retold with the same reverence as the
gospel stories, but dramatic presentations continue to reflect
upon the liberating power that she is capable of transmitting
to her children. It continues to fascinate believers and un-
believers alike. It continues to draw together peoples of all
backgrounds — rich and poor, Mexican and U.S., white and
brown, Protestant and Catholic. She is a sacred icon whose
power is far beyond our abilities of comprehension but whose
life-giving power and liberating influence are at the very core
of our untiring struggles for survival and new life.

From Death to New Life

I do not know of any other event in the history of Christianity that stands at the very source of the birth of a people
like the appearance of Our Lady of Guadalupe. One cannot
know, understand, or appreciate the Mexican people without
a deep appreciation of Guadalupe. Equally, one cannot appreciate the full salvific and redemptive force of Guadalupe
without seeing it in the full context of the historical moment
in which it took place. Guadalupe is not just an apparition,
but a major intervention of God's liberating power in history. It is an Exodus and Resurrection event of an enslaved
and dying people. The God of freedom liberates from the
strongest possible government and this same God of life raises
to new life what human beings seek to kill. Guadalupe is
truly an epiphany of God's love at the precise moment when
abandonment by God had been experienced by the people at
large.

Were it not for Our Lady of Guadalupe, there would be no
Mexican and no Mexican-American people today. The great
Mexican nations had been defeated by the Spanish invasion

that came to a violent and bloody climax in 1521. The native peoples who had not been killed no longer wanted to live. Everything of value to them, including their religion, had been desecrated or destroyed. Nothing made sense any more. Nothing was worth living for. With this colossal catastrophe, their entire past became irrelevant. New diseases appeared and together with the trauma of the collective death-wish of the people, the native population decreased drastically.

The Mexicans had been a well-developed and proud people. Now they were condemned to a subservient existence. The new masters had taken over and imposed a totally new system — new rulers, new ways of life, new language, and even a new religion. The missioners, kindly and saintly as they were, were nevertheless the ultimate legitimating agents of the new way of life. Hence, from the Mexican perspective, they were the ones to give the final blow of death to the Mexican way of life by seeking to uproot and kill their religion. Physical violence by the conquistadors destroyed their entire way of life, and religious violence through the activity of the missioners made life not only impossible but undesirable. It was better not to live at all. It was better to die.

It is in this climate of the stench and the cries of death that the new and unsuspected beginning would take place. Like the resurrection itself, it came at the moment when everything appeared to be finished. The old native ways had been crushed. There seemed to be no possibility whatsoever of future life. The Guadalupe story, like the stories of the Gospels, is very simple and child-like. Yet the full meaning of its imagery, movements, persons, and words is still to be discovered. I contend that it is the first real anthropological translation and proclamation of the gospel to the people of the Americas. That is why, upon seeing and hearing, millions responded in faith.

First "Evangelium" of the Americas

The elements of the Guadalupe story are as simple as they are beautiful. Early on the morning of December 9, 1531, a middle-aged Indian by the name of Juan Diego was on his way to mass at the church of Tlatelolco. As he passed by the edge of the small hill of Tepeyac, he was astounded to hear the most beautiful singing of precious birds. It was so beautiful that he thought he must be dreaming or be in paradise. Suddenly a beautiful lady, whose clothes radiated like the sun, appeared and called him by his name in a most endearing way.

She then spoke to him and made known her will:

Know and understand, you the dearest of my children, that I am the every holy Virgin Mary, mother of the true God through whom one lives, of the creator of heaven and earth. I have a living desire that there be built a temple, so that in it I can show and give forth all my love, compassion, help, and defense, because I am your loving mother: to you, to all who are with you, to all the inhabitants of this land and to all who love me, call upon me, and trust in me, I will hear their lamentations and will remedy all their miseries, pains, and sufferings.

In order to bring about what my mercy intends, go to the palace of the bishop and tell him how I have sent you to manifest to him what I very much desire, that here on this site below the hill, a temple be built to me.

Without hesitation, Juan Diego was immediately on his way. As could be expected he had difficulty in getting to see the bishop. When he finally got the desired audience, the bishop listened, but it was evident that he did not believe him.

Having been rejected by the bishop, Juan Diego returned to the lady with feelings of nothingness and unworthiness. He begged her to get someone better qualified and more trustworthy to be her messenger. But the lady insisted:

> Listen, my son, the dearest of my children, I want you to understand that I have many servants and messengers to whom I can entrust this message, but in every aspect it is precisely my desire that you be my entrusted messenger, that through your mediation my wish may be fulfilled. Tomorrow, go to see the bishop and once again tell him that I personally, the very holy Virgin Mary, Mother of God, sends you.

The next day, Juan Diego went as instructed. Once again he had difficulty getting to see the bishop. This time the bishop listened with more interest, but asked him to ask his lady from heaven for a sign that the bishop might believe. Juan Diego assured the bishop he would bring the sign and immediately set out to tell the lady. She assured him that tomorrow morning she would have the sign for him. However, when he arrived home, he discovered his uncle, Juan Bernardino, to be gravely ill. So the next morning, instead of going for the sign, he set out through a different route to find the priest that could come anoint his uncle. But the Lady appeared to him and assured him that his uncle was well and that he was to go to the top of the hill where he would find the sign the bishop asked for. He immediately ran to the top of the hill where he discovered beautiful roses of all colors.

He filled his *tilma,* or cloak, with the flowers and rushed to the bishop's palace with his great prize. When he was finally admitted into the bishop's office, in the presence of the bishop and his curia, Juan Diego unfolded his *tilma.* As all were admiring the beautiful roses, which were totally exceptional during December, the image of the Lady appeared on the *tilma* of Juan Diego and has remained there ever since. From that moment on, millions of Mexicans have come to the church through the mediation of the brown virgin of Tepeyac.

To appreciate the meaning of the story, it is necessary to see it through the categories of the ancient Nahuatl language — a language that expresses ultimate reality through image and poetry. The story begins with the *beautiful singing of the birds* and ends with *exquisite flowers*. For the native world, the expression for a divine message was precisely flower and song. Thus the entire story happens within the realm of a divine revelation: not from human beings but from God.

The lady hides *the sun* but does not extinguish it. This is most important, for the missionaries were trying to destroy everything of the native religion as diabolical. She is greater than the natives' greatest manifestation of the deity, the sun, but she does not destroy it. She will transcend, but not do away with. This is the assurance that their ancient way of life will continue, but now reinterpreted through something new and greater. She is standing upon *the moon* and therefore superior to their second greatest manifestation of the deity.

She wears the *turquoise* mantle. Turquoise was the color reserved for the supreme deity, who alone could bring harmonious unity out of the opposing forces that governed the universe. Her dress was the *pale red* of the blood sacrifices. She had assumed the blood sacrifices of her people and was now in turn offering herself to her people. She appears with hands folded over her heart and pointed in the direction of the people — the native sign of the offering of self to others.

She who was greater than all their divinities was herself not a goddess, for she wore no mask and *her eyes* were beautiful. In her eyes, the image of a person is easily discerned. In her eyes, every generation of Mexicans has seen themselves personally accepted, respected, loved, and valued. There is nothing more life-giving than to see ourselves reflected, accepted, and valued in the eyes of an important other. In the very gaze of the eye there is rebirth.

This beautiful lady who is truly from above and yet very much one of their own is pregnant, for she wears the *waist band of maternity.* Furthermore, over her womb, one finds the ancient Aztec glyph for the center of the universe. Thus she, according to ancient Nahuatl cosmology, has assumed the five previous ages — called suns — and is now the sign of the sixth age. What she offers to the world she carries within her womb: the new center of the universe about to be full born in the Americas. Through the lady millions would approach the church for Christian instruction and baptism.

Beginning of the New Race

The natives who previously had wanted only to die now wanted to live; dances, songs, pilgrimages, and festivities resumed! A new life began. The immediate socio-political structure was not changed, but there was now an unsuspected foundation for a new future. In the beginning, the church opposed the new devotion, but the people promulgated and celebrated it. It spread like a wildfire propelled by high winds. Eventually the church joined, and in time even the pope came to venerate the new mother of all the inhabitants of the Americas.

At the end of an era, at the sanctuary of the ancient mother of this earth, arose the new mother of the *mestizo* generations to come. Races and nations had been opposed to each other, but as the mother of all the inhabitants of these lands, she would provide the basis for a new unity. It is not surprising that this event took place early in the morning, at the first signs of the new day, for it was the beginning of the New Day of the Americas. It was the sunrise service of the Americas.

She came from this soil. She did not come to undo the events of the past and return to "the good old days," for that never happens. But she did come to bring something new out of the chaotic events of the past. She is neither an Indian goddess nor a European Madonna; she is something new. She is neither Spanish nor Indian and yet she is both and more; she is inviting and not threatening; she unites what others strive to divide. She is the first truly American person and as such the mother of the new generations to come. In her children divisions of race and nationality will be overcome, the downtrodden will be uplifted, the marginated will be welcomed home, the cries of the silenced will be heard, and the dying will come to new life.

But beyond all my explanation and the pious or cynical interpretations of others, the power and force of the devotion continues to increase throughout the Americas. In any major city in the United States the 12th of December is celebrated each year with the greatest joy and solemnity. It is commemorated with processions, dances, songs, presentations of the original experience, masses, crownings. The impact of her presence attracts the masses of the faithful, but it equally attracts the attentions of theologians, historians, and scientists. It is not an event that happened only some 450 years ago, but an event that continues to transform millions of people throughout the Americas today. The full meaning of Guadalupe cannot be adequately explained, but it can be experienced.

Guadalupe has a magnetic power to attract diverse people from all walks of life and, in her, they can experience unity. The basis of this unity is not the feeling that one often has at large gatherings, that of being absorbed by the mob. The deepest basis of the humanizing unity is that regardless of the magnitude of the crowds, in her presence, each individual experiences personal recognition. Each one is looked upon compassionately eye-to-eye and tenderly called

by name. Thus Guadalupe is the experience (not the il-
lusion) of family, of community and individuality, in the
midst of a world of anonymity and division. In spite of the
threats of death, Guadalupe is an experience and guarantee
of life.

Chapter 6

Galilee of Mestizos

Is Human Liberation Possible?

Along with many of my people, I too was searching for answers. There were no doubts that our people had been oppressed and exploited by church and society alike. There were no doubts that we had to work not only for deep change and human progress, but for a total liberation that would result in a new creation. But as the movements started to advance, the questions did not disappear. On the contrary, they deepened and expanded. New advances presented new problems. One nationally recognized psychiatrist, Dr. Roberto Jiménez, who himself is a product of the barrio, has often stated that it seems that to the degree that Mexican-Americans advance in life, they disintegrate personally. Archbishop Flores and I, who have been involved in the struggle since the very beginning, experienced the rapid disintegration of much of our way of life. We were advancing politically and economically, but humanly speaking we seemed to be going backward. Often it seemed as if we were losing the best traits of our Mexican heritage and assuming the worst of the U.S.A. There was deep frustration among the leadership of our people. It was almost as if the struggle for human progress was an exercise in human futility.

I searched for answers in many places, but never did I imagine that I would discover the deepest and most far-reaching answer in the very person of Jesus. From my earliest memories, it was in Jesus and in *Nuestra Señora de Guadalupe* that our people found comfort and strength. How happy I was when I made my first communion at the age of five or six because my grandmother assured me that henceforth I would never be alone for Jesus would always be with me. That knowledge has always been a source of strength for me. In him, our people have discovered that meaning which is beyond the power of worldly reason to comprehend. Yet the more I entered into contemporary society, the more this fundamental conviction faded into my subconscious.

I have been very religious-minded all my life and also very civic-minded. In my family, going to Sunday mass was as much a sacred obligation as was getting involved in the movements for the betterment of our people. Yet, the two activities had never been connected. Religion had to do with God: doctrine, morals, sin, repentance, prayer, mass, the sacraments, and life in the hereafter. Surely there were many beautiful life-values taught: forgiveness of one another; helping others, especially those in need; love, even of one's enemies (although loving the immediate neighbor was often more difficult). Civic activities had to do with the affairs of the world. They were important, for God had given us the world to cultivate and take care of, but they did not seem to be part of the immediate concerns of religion.

I would often hear fundamentalists say, "Jesus is the answer," and "Jesus saves," but in my own simplistic way, I applied it only to vagabonds, beggars, winos, derelicts, and street people in general. The rest of us good religious folks, rich or poor, Anglo or Mexican-American, were already among the saved. All we had to do now was better our lot in life by dedication and hard work. To speak about Jesus seemed so fundamentalistic, pious, simplistic, and even anti-intellectual. The fundamentalists could speak about Jesus, while we "smarter folks" in the established churches spoke about theology. They had stories about Jesus but we had the doctrines and dogmas of the faith. We had more important things to speak about, like the church, the commandments, and the sacraments. Jesus, sad to say, we took for granted — and, in effect, ignored. We were concerned with the customs, structures, and teachings of the church, but not with the proclamation and celebration of his memory. His personal presence was distant from us, but we did not even realize it because he was sacramentally present in the tabernacle. Ironically, the overassurance of his sacramental presence often obscured his personal presence. And worse yet, we seemed afraid to really speak about him and get to know him personally.

Yet the masses of our simple folk, not encumbered with the complexity of the philosophical formulations of the faith of the educated elite, kept the faith because of their personal knowledge and relationship with *Papacito Dios,* Jesus, Mary, and the saints. Their ignorance of the so-called truths of the faith enabled them to know very well the foundation of all the theologically and doctrinally elaborated truth: the person of Jesus the Lord. Others knew a lot about him, but the poor folks knew him personally. For them, he was not a theory or a doctrine, but a living person — a friend, an older brother, the "master" who — unlike the masters of this world who abused, exploited, and insulted us — was always solicitous for our welfare and would always be around to help us and comfort us on our way.

This personal knowledge of the Lord, which was so much a part of my inner being and of that of my people, was eclipsed for a brief period of my life. By the time I was in college, and more so in seminary, I had many philosophical questions about the nature of the human being and the natural quest of humanity for happiness. They were real but abstract

questions about the essence of human existence. In my theological studies I read about God's revelation in Christ as the
answer to every human question — not just the answers to
the questions that we ask, but the answer to the question of
our existence. The revelation of Christ correlates with the
great aspirations of the human heart that were placed there
by the Creator. It corresponds to the deepest yearning of the
human spirit. I had no trouble accepting this in the universal
sense, but little did I realize that it also applies beautifully
to the very specific and particular question that the Mexican-
American is.

Many of our people had been making all-out efforts to save
ourselves from poverty, misery, and ignorance. We had been
trying to come out of the hellish cycle of poverty to which we
had been condemned for so many generations. Yet, in coming out, we often jumped into other forms of enslavement.
What should be the direction of our efforts? Some looked
toward the economic programs of Washington, others toward
the revolutionary movements of Latin America, still others
toward the ideological theories of Europe. Yet there seemed
to be no satisfactory way. Something more was desperately
needed. It had to be beyond the ideological, the economic,
or the political. It had to offer something new both culturally
and socially. It had to give us new ways of looking at reality
and new ways of speaking about our faith, which was the very
basis of our existence. The Euro-American ways of the established church were not the ways of our people. The clergy,
religious, and theologians were still foreigners and strangers
to our way of life and to our expressions of the faith. Their
language of God did not reflect our experience of God and
their priorities of church life did not reflect our experience of
church. We had to articulate, proclaim, and sing the praises
of the Lord of life in ways that were truly native and natural
to our people.

We needed to discover a new spirit that would move us

all beyond the death-pains of conquest and domination to the spirit of liberty and harmony. But the world is so entrenched in the spirit of the survival and superiority of the strongest that it seems that the only way of surviving and truly becoming someone is by taking over the positions of power. Yet when this happens nothing really changes and humanity simply continues on the road of conquest and domination.

For too long the radically liberating way of Jesus had been hidden behind the façade of Christendom, which has tended to confuse the powers and glories of this world with the power and glory of the risen Lord. Since the time of Constantine, the church has been more interested in defending its worldly powers than the liberation of the imprisoned and oppressed of the world. Certainly there have always been exceptions, but they were just that — exceptions. It has not been infrequent in the history of the church for the powers of the earthly Christian kingdoms to be confused and equated with the powers of the gospel. In the name of the gospel, cultures have been imposed upon entire nations and different races have been conquered, annihilated, or enslaved as worthless heathens. In the name of defending the law and order of the nation, the church has often stood by silently as the nothings of society have been exploited and deported.

In my Christian faith, I knew that Jesus was our Savior and that he was the Savior of the world. But never did I imagine that the way of Jesus of Nazareth would be such a clear road map leading us to a true salvation that begins right now in this world as soon as we recognize it and accept it as the way. The way of Jesus leads us from confusion to clarity, from enslavement to freedom, from death to life. I never imagined that Jesus would have so much to offer, concretely speaking, to the great Mexican-American question — to the quest for life, liberty, justice, equality, and true happiness.

Conquest or Birth

During the year I spent in Paris studying at the Institute Catholique and living with the Jesuit Fathers, I fell in love with France and the ways of the French people. I made many lasting friends and I always look forward to opportunities for visiting. Yet there was one very painful experience during my stay in France: the language. I had never really spoken French before and the struggle of trying to speak it and quite often not being understood brought back to mind my early boyhood experiences with the English language. Once again I relived the shame and frustration of not understanding and even worse of not being understood. Often there was a deep loneliness because of the inability to communicate. This experience helped me to come into much closer contact with the contemporary situation of many of my people who because of linguistic difficulties often remain ignorant of the simplest instructions and remain silent because of the fear of being ridiculed. I had forgotten how important language is to the sense of belonging and well-being.

As I was working on my doctoral dissertation on *mestizaje* in Paris, I kept struggling to find a connection between what appeared to be two theses that did not connect: the socio-historical process of the twofold *mestizaje* of Mexican-Americans and the socio-historical identity and mission of Jesus. In Jesus, God had become a particular man at a specific moment of time in a determined portion of the globe. Some unidentified inner drive kept pushing me to discover a connection between Jesus and our own situation. Intuitively I felt it was there.

Since the great challenge of Pope John XXIII to rediscover that which is essential to Christianity, my own fascination with a return to our Christian roots had been increasing. This had projected me into a rediscovery of the originality and dynamism of the way of Jesus, and, even more, of the socio-cultural person of Jesus himself. If in the man Jesus we saw God, who is life itself, then who was this Jesus?

The reality and function of *mestizaje* had been gradually emerging. During the summer of 1968 I was flying from Medellín, Colombia, to Miami with Professor Jacques Audinet from Paris, who had delivered one of the key addresses at the International Catechetical Congress. As we were flying over Mexico, he told me how he had been captivated by the monument to "La Raza" in Mexico City and especially by an inscription on the site of the final battles between Cortés and the Indian nations: "Neither a defeat nor a victory, but the painful birth of the *mestizo* people that is Mexico today." From the categories of conquest to those of birth.

From a realization of the uniqueness of the Mexican *mestizo,* as proclaimed in that inscription at the Plaza de las Tres Culturas in Mexico City, I moved to a discovery of the new *mestizaje* of the Southwest that was pulling Anglos and Mexican-Americans alike into the formation of a new humanity. As some would say, this was the emergence of the new cultural nation of *Mexiamérica.* As I consciously rewalked the historical pilgrimage, no longer through the categories of conquest but through the categories of birth, I saw the identity of the new being in a new light.

Sometimes I thought I should just develop one or the other of the two emerging theses and just keep the other one as a subject of personal interest. But my inner self rebelled against that. Through frustration coupled with occasional emptiness and even anger, the all-important element started to come into focus: my unquestioned experience-based knowledge that Jesus was my life, my hope, and my liberation; he was the source of the strength and survival of the people and would now be the source of liberation. I was finally able to verbalize what intuitively I had known all along.

The Unimagined Liberation

The earliest Gospel, Mark, begins with words that echo the beginning of the creation narrative in Genesis: "In the beginning..." "Here begins...." From the first words of the Gospel we are given the clue for proper understanding: here is a new and unsuspected beginning. It is not a reform or a renewal, but the eruption of something totally new. The world had become so confused in its own mechanisms of sin that it was impossible to know truth, and especially the truth about persons. Values and cultures of the world seemed constantly to find ways of degrading and ostracizing persons, peoples, and nations so that the victims of injustice appeared as unworthy public sinners while the criminals appeared as the noble pillars of society. People battled against one another to such incredible degrees that the jungles seemed far more civilized than human civilization. As St. Paul said: "there is no one who understands, no one in search of God. All have taken the wrong course, all alike have become worthless" (Rom. 3:11–12).

In the midst of this confusion, an experience of good news suddenly began among the poor and destitute of society. One of the marginated ones now became the source of solidarity and messianic hope among the masses of hopeless people. He was no well-intentioned outsider or missioner. Out of the ranks of the nobodies of the world, one of their own became the source of friendship, community, and hope. This is the core of the *evangelium*.

This "good news" from among the poor is clearly brought out in one of the first proclamations of Peter, the leader of the new group: "The stone which was rejected by the builders has become the cornerstone" (Acts 4:11). This stone rejected by the builders of the empires and even by the pious and upright people of the old world order is Jesus, the man who came from Nazareth, a town in Galilee. As Mark states: *Here begins the Good News.* The first creation marked the beginning of time; now in time, the new, definitive, and eternal creation begins.

I had always known Jesus Christ to be the Savior of the world, the eternally begotten Son of God, the one who died and was resurrected and is seated at the right hand of the Father. I had enjoyed his teachings and marveled at his miracles. I had agonized with his passion and death and rejoiced during the Easter season — mainly because the Lenten sacrifices and penances had come to an end.

As I tried to reconstruct his way, a previously unquestioned aspect started to emerge: his earthly identity. Humanly speaking, just who was this Jesus of Nazareth? It seemed like such an elementary question, but I had never asked it before, nor had I found it studied seriously in any of the works on Christ that I knew of. His socio-cultural identity was simply passed by or idealized into a heavenly existence. The fullness of the Incarnation was not appreciated, and in many ways we Christians are still scandalized by just how human our God became. Through some kind of unidentified fear, the Western world and its theologians seem to have been afraid of dealing with the real earthly identity of Jesus. It is almost as if the West would like to say, "Confess Christ but forget Jesus," the real Jesus who walked our earth, ate our food, and suffered the injustices of our world.

All the dogmas of our Christian tradition take on a far richer signification when we appreciate the socio-cultural reality through which the events of our salvation have taken place. The more we appreciate the humanity of the Scriptures, the more we appreciate their divinity. For after all, God chose to work through human agents and human situations to bring about the rehabilitation of the human race. And I go even further. Only to the degree that we appreciate the humanity of the Scriptures, and especially of Jesus, will we truly see, hear, and know the God that Jesus sought to make known to us. Distance from the full humanity of Jesus is distance from the God made known in and through Jesus.

We know that in Jesus, God became a poor man that we might become rich, but just how poor he really became continues to be as shocking as it is scandalous. Yet the God of the Bible is always full of unsuspected surprises in favor of the lowly, the marginated, and the disinherited of the world.

What passport would he have carried? What kind of accent did he speak with? How was he looked upon by his contemporaries? What kind of reaction would his ethnic and racial characteristics have caused in those of the dominant classes of his day? If God really became man, then God neither did become nor could become universal man, for universal man does not exist. God had to become a historically, culturally, and racially determined man. Just who was that man that was, according to our Christian beliefs, the God-made-man for our salvation?

Is not his earthly identity the very first revelation? Is not this the first image that each one of us presents of ourselves — like it or not? Is this not the first impression that others get of us, even before really knowing us? We react and judge in a prejudiced way in accordance with our stereotypes of others.

He was a Jew. But the Jewish people themselves referred to him as a Galilean. Even though Galilee does not appear as an important designation in the Old Testament, the Jews and the early Christians made a point of referring to Jesus as a Galilean. The Galilean identity of Jesus and of his first followers is one of the constants of the New Testament.

As I started to explore the socio-cultural imagery of Galilee I became more intrigued. It was a borderland, the great border region between the Greeks and the Jews of Judea. People of all nationalities came along the caravan routes on their way to and from Egypt. There was abundant agriculture and commerce and a flourishing Greek society. The Jews were in the minority and were forced to mix with their gentile neighbors. It was a land of great mixture and of an ongoing *mestizaje* — similar to our own Southwest of the United States. The Galilean Jews spoke with a very marked accent and most likely mixed their language quite readily with the Greek of the dominant culture and the Latin of the Roman Empire. Peter could deny Jesus, but there was no way he could deny he was a Galilean. The moment he opened his mouth he revealed his Galilean identity.

The more I discovered about Galilee, the more I felt at home there and the more Jesus truly became my flesh-and-blood brother. He was not just a religious icon, but a living partner in the human struggle for life. He too had lived the experience of human distance and ridicule. Being a Jew in Galilee was very much like being a Mexican-American in Texas. As the Jews in Galilee were too Jewish to be accepted by the gentile population and too contaminated with pagan ways to be accepted by the pure-minded Jews of Jerusalem, so have the Mexican-Americans in the Southwest been rejected by two groups.

I had often made the confession of faith: "Conceived by the Holy Spirit and born of the Virgin Mary." I have never questioned this. Yet, I had never wondered how the people of his times saw his origins. In the Gospel of Luke, the angel appeared to Mary and to Mary alone. In Matthew's Gospel it is evident that Joseph was scandalized that Mary was with child and wanted to put her away. I wonder what the town gossip was like? Just who was the father of Jesus? There must have been plenty of stories going around.

Jesus had been conceived in Galilee, a land of many Roman soldiers. They easily took the native women to bed; some went freely and others were forced. Is this not the way of all military forces? Of all conquering soldiers? The conquest of the local women is the ultimate sign of conquering power, the ultimate humiliation of the women who are abused and of the men who can do nothing about what is happen-

ing. Are not the children of American soldiers who carried on
this ancient military tradition in Vietnam still searching for
identity and acceptance, whether in Vietnam or the United
States? Will not the children being born of U.S. soldiers in
Honduras today face the same trauma? Was not the father of
Jesus a Roman soldier? This would certainly have been suspected by those who knew Mary. Early rumors to this effect
persisted during the first three hundred years of the Christian
movement. It must have been painful for Mary and later on
for Jesus to have to deal with these stories. It is not what
we really are that we have to live with but with what people
around us say that we are. And once a rumor is started, even
if it is fabricated and without any shade of truth, it can still
stain the person for life.

Suddenly the miraculous conception of Jesus and the vir-
ginity of Mary became one of the most vibrant aspects of
my faith. The fact that Jesus had been conceived by the
Holy Spirit meant that the people did not know how he had
been conceived. According to human standards, he was of
doubtful origins, and thus by reason of his very birth he entered into solidarity with the masses whose origins are questioned by those in power. As a human being, he did not
have to enter into solidarity with the destitute and rejected
of the world — because he was born one of them. The world
might consider him illegitimate, but God would proclaim him
God's own beloved son: rejected by the world, but chosen by
God.

Mary and Joseph had to travel to the town of their origins.
Yet there was no room for them in their own territory, quite
possibly because Galileans were despised in Judea. After the
birth of the child, they once again had to migrate, this time
to Egypt, where they would live as foreigners during the early
formative years of the life of Jesus. Migrations and social
distance would be the core of the daily life of Jesus. He knew
by experience the suffering and pain of living in a foreign land

and even of being considered an outcast in his own home territory.

By growing up in Galilee, Jesus was a cultural *mestizo,* assuming unto himself the great traditions that flourished in his home territory. No matter how much we resist, we become the traditions of the area in which we live. This is a fact of life. Culturally and linguistically speaking, Jesus was a *mestizo.* And we dare say that to those of his time, he must have even appeared to be a biological *mestizo* — the child of a Jewish girl and a Roman father. Rumors even circulated that the name of the child's father was Panthera. No wonder the pure-minded Jews hated him and became indignant when Pilate proclaimed him king of the Jews. He appeared to be "contaminated" to the deepest core of his existence. He appeared to be a half-breed. A scandal to all the pious and the pure of society. How could such a one be their savior and king? Yet this scandalous beginning is the root of the essential catholicity of his movement, of his church.

Jesus is thus the rejected one who becomes the source of solidarity among the rejected of society. Through him, with him, and in him, the prostitutes, the tax collectors, the Samaritans (who stand for the rejected and despised neighbor), the public sinners of society, and all *hoi polloi* passed from being a faceless and nameless mass of individuals to a community of friends. Their state in life had not changed, but they had changed in that which ultimately makes a difference: their relationships of love between one another. They were no longer nobodies but were now important to one another. With the stone that was rejected, the rejected of the world began to build a new human edifice into which all others — ordinary poor, middle class, and even the rich and the powerful — would later want to come.

No wonder they kept saying, "What good can come out of Galilee? . . . This man is possessed by the chief of demons."

How could such a no-good person be a source of anything good? In his existence, Jesus was the antithesis of all human quests for "purity," which in effect lead to segregation, degradation, exploitation, and death.

This aspect of the beginning of the salvific mission of Jesus has become liberating to me personally, and it has become one of the key themes of my preaching and teaching. The people always react with enthusiastic surprise and even with tears of joy. For in speaking about the lowly condition of Jesus, our own social distance and loneliness take on a new meaning. The Son of God made man for our salvation is no longer a mighty, powerful, and distant other, as all the important people of society and even church have been for us; rather he is one of our own who lived the same violence and social distance that we have been subjected to. If this condition characterized the very beginning of Christ's redemptive mission to the world, then our own historical and cultural status must have some important role in God's historical project for humanity. It may not be suspected by the world, but in Jesus it is clearly made known to us.

When the Epistle to the Philippians says that Jesus became nothing, it is no mere figure of speech. In a very existential way, he became the nothing of all human groups — the *mestizo* whose existence is the nonexistence of permanent exclusion. No matter where you go or where you are, you are never fully accepted because you are the other.

The quest for human purity defines boundaries and very quickly excludes those who have been the product of territorial transgression. There seems to be an inner fear that the children of territorial transgression pose the deepest threat to the existence of the group and to the survival of its purity, with its well-defined boundaries of acceptability and belonging. Thus the *mestizo* becomes the one rejected by all, the truly nothing of this world.

In becoming man, why would God begin by becoming a

mestizo? St. Paul gives us a clue when in 1 Corinthians 1 he states that it has pleased God to choose the nothings of this world — the low class, the unimportant, those who count for nothing. St. Peter, in one of his first sermons, states that the stone that has been rejected by the builders of this world has been chosen by God to become the cornerstone of the new creation.

But one does not have to be a *mestizo* to be considered as low-class or as nothing. Why then is the *mestizaje* of Jesus redemptive?

Jesus himself tells us that he came that all might be one. The miracle of Pentecost is the unity of all nations. Divisions, whether among individuals, among nations, or among races, are the curse of the sin of the world. God created us that even in our differences we might enrich one another. Linguistic, racial, and cultural differences are not meant to be a source of division, but elements of a universal harmony. In Genesis 9 and 10 the great diversity of clans, languages, and nations is presented as a sign of God's creative blessing.

Yet it seems to be part of the sinful condition of humanity that we consistently seek to divide one another. And even worse, we try to become someone by stepping upon others and even destroying them so that we might advance. Superiority rather than fraternity seems to be the rule of humanity's quest for happiness. Thus brothers and sisters, families, clans, nations, and races are posed one against the other. As one gets into power, barriers of all types are built up so that others will not get in. Nations set up borders, and "superior" races set up codes so that their sacred territory will not be invaded — whether it be geographical, psychological, biological, or religious territory. The toughest boundaries to cross are frequently the religious. Marriage becomes an all-important institution in protecting the boundaries and interests of the group. Thus parents want children to marry within their own group of acceptability.

It is true that love breaks all boundaries, but it does not do away with racial and cultural differences. Mixed marriages are possible, but they are not easy, especially when the differences are religious ones. Religious differences are the most difficult to overcome, for they tend to form almost absolute barriers. The child who is born of parents of diverse groups is often ostracized and rejected. *Mestizaje* seems to be one of the universal taboos. Yet it is a most natural ongoing process. *Mestizo* children can be quite beautiful because they receive from the genes of both parents, and quite intelligent because they are enriched by the traditions of both parents. Yet they are looked down upon as half-breeds, as not fully belonging, as nothing, by much of society.

From Margination to Unity

Jesus became existential nothingness. He came that all might be one, and it is precisely by breaking all the barriers at the deepest level of human existence that he himself in his very person initiates the new existence. This beginning in highly *mestizo* Galilee will become the cultural basis of his mission. There he will learn not just from his Jewish faith, but from the many traditions that enriched his home territory. There territorial distances had to be transgressed in order to live and survive. There differences simply blended in. There, far away from all the centers of defined belonging, one could easily make a new beginning without even realizing it was happening.

Jesus assumes the suffering of margination and rejection, not to consecrate it as good in and for itself, for that would be a type of segregation. Because division and separation have been the sin of the world, he assumes the pain of becoming the rejected one of such a sinful society so that from within he may begin his mission: the unity of the human family. Having suffered the pain of rejection, he rejects rejection and gives us the bases for the restructuring of all society. We are all invited to be children in the Reign of God.

What matters is not our nationality, religion, or family name, but that we live God's will (Mark 3:35). It is that response alone that now becomes the basis of the new human family that transcends and pierces through *all* human boundaries. We can all form a new human family, not because of what we have been in the past, but because of how we respond today to God's invitation to universal and universalizing love.

But Jesus does not proclaim some sort of new ideology. He lives out a new alternative, not by fighting against anyone or even by defending the ways of his religion. He proclaims the Reign of God, teaches about God's way of life for all humanity, and most of all dares to live what others fear: the joy of common table fellowship with everyone. By freely eating with everyone, he breaks and challenges all the social taboos that keep people apart.

The most earth-shaking activity of the Jesus revolution of human standards was his unquestioned joy of table fellowship with everyone and anyone. Some feel that it was this, which so scandalized all the good and religious people of his times, that sent him to the cross the fastest. Jesus lived and died for what he believed in. And in his death-resurrection, we have been given the power to do likewise. The first followers of Jesus continued that which had been most original to Jesus: the table fellowship for all people. For it was precisely in the celebration of the fellowship that old barriers, while not disappearing, would nevertheless no longer serve as barriers. In the fellowship, persons of very diverse and even antagonistic backgrounds discovered a new source of unity, understanding, and love. From the experience of table fellowship, new forms of fellowship in everyday life would gradually be formulated.

It is in the fiestas of life that we break down human barriers of separation; this has been our experience in the Mexican-American community. It is in our fiestas that we transcend divisions and experience new unity. It is in the great Fiesta of San Antonio that all San Antonio transcends the barriers that still divide us and celebrate what has indeed begun — even if it is not yet fully realized.

In his *mestizo* existence Jesus breaks the barriers of separation, as does every *mestizo,* and already begins to live a new unity. That is both the threat and the greatness of a *mestizo* existence. *Mestizos* may struggle to become one or the other of the great traditions out of which they are born, but even if they were to succeed, that would be a mere return to the previous divisions of society. We usher in new life for the betterment of everyone when we freely and consciously assume the great traditions flowing through our veins and transcend them, not by denying either but by synthesizing them into something new.

The *mestizo* is the biblical stone, rejected by the builders of this world, that God has chosen to be the cornerstone of a new creation, not chosen for honor and privilege, but for a sacred mission. Having been marginated and misunderstood, we know the suffering of separation by our own experience; we know that this type of existence is wrong and it must change. But change does not mean that we now take over and impose our ways upon all. This would simply be a new conquest, a new domination, and nothing would really change. The *mestizo* affirms both the identities received while offering something new to both. Being an inside-outsider and an outside-insider to two worlds at the same time, we have the unique privilege of seeing and appreciating both worlds. It is from this position that we begin to combine the elements of both to form something new.

In the *mestizaje* and mission of Jesus our own *mestizaje* is transformed and redeemed. What appeared to be a curse to some now appears for what it truly is — a blessing. What humanly speaking is the basis of margination and rejection is now discovered to be the basis of divine election. What appeared to be at the furthest outposts of the frontiers of nationality and race, now is recognized as the cradle of a new humanity. In Jesus, our curse has become blessing, our rejection has become election, and our margination has become the center of a new humanity. For us, this has been an experience of resurrection, a paschal experience of passing through death to life to new existence.

Jesus did not give in to the fashion of many of the educated Jews of his time by assuming the ways of Greek culture, but neither did he simply affirm and purify his Jewish ways. He offered a new alternative to both and through them to everybody else. It is in this new alternative that all the previous traditions are assumed and transcended. Thus it is in the very way of Jesus that *mestizos* find their mission: to create. In this is both the excitement and the challenge. God might have created the world in seven days, but it takes us many generations to create a new humanity, a new culture. It cannot be merely legislated. It has to develop gradually through the efforts of the poets, the artists, the thinkers, the artisans. The care and cultivation of "this earth," that is, of this portion of the globe in which we are blending with others to move from a society of multiple barriers of division to a newly created society of unity, will take generations of daring dreams and heroic struggles.

It is in the identity and mission of Jesus, as they functioned in his own day and times, that I find the answer to the riddle of the real and ultimate identity and struggles of Mexican-Americans. It is in his way that our own way becomes clarified, and the direction of our efforts is oriented. We will never rise to the full potential of our being by way of denial. It is through the full acceptance of our past that we will be able to live freely today and truly transcend it tomorrow.

As Jesus is the Savior of all peoples, he is the personal savior of the Mexican-American people as he speaks directly to the deepest level of our human suffering and to our most fervent aspirations. His way liberates us from false aspirations and opens up unimagined possibilities. He liberates us by giving a totally new signification to our identity and a challenging mission to our movements. In him, curse is transformed into blessing and rejection becomes election for a sacred mission.

It is not just an abstract or universal liberation, but an existential one, for he has become the light of our socio-historical world and the one who is liberating us from the cultural enslavements of our time and space. He is the good news that has turned our despair into hope, our darkness into light, our confusion into clear knowledge, our pain into happiness, our sorrow into joy, and our old life into the beginning of new life.

Chapter 7

Toward Universal Mestizaje

The future begins in the dream of what could and ought to be. When they are first announced, such dreams often appear as naive, simplistic, impossible, destructive of good order, and heretical. Yet dreams are the sparks of discoveries that allow us to transcend the barriers of present-day limitations of life. At one time, a democratic republic composed of free citizens was but a dream. It even appeared to some to be a violation of the natural laws of governance. Yet dreamers dared to convert their dreams into living forms, and today we have the democratic model of the United States of America and many other democratic forms of government.

In the midst of invasion and great national crisis, the prophet Isaiah dared to dream that someday all nations would come to the mountain of the Lord and would "beat their swords into plowshares and their spears into pruning hooks; one nation shall not raise the sword against another, nor shall they train for war again" (Isa. 2:3–5). In the midst of destructive wars, he could dream of a time of peace when even the wild animals of the field would become friends: "Then the wolf shall be a guest of the lamb, and the leopard shall lie down with the kid; the calf and the young lion shall browse together with a little child to guide them.... There shall be no harm or ruin on all my holy mountain; for the earth shall be filled with the knowledge of the Lord as the water covers the seas" (Isa. 11).

Out of the suffering of the divided and segregated society of his times, Jesus too ushered in a new reality and proclaimed the dream "that all may be one" (John 17:21). He died for that dream, yet on the morning of Pentecost the dream began to be realized and many diverse peoples were able to experience a new family unity that transcended many of the old barriers that had kept them apart. Simón Bolívar had a dream of a united America without national borders; it has not yet been realized, but it is still a great dream. Martin Luther King, Jr., had a dream, whose realization has begun, but it will be a long time before it will be completed.

We cannot just adjust the models of society to alleviate some of the suffering; we must dream of creating new models wherein the very roots of the suffering will be eliminated. It is the greatness of the human spirit not to give in to suffering or merely to accept it as inevitable, but within the suffering itself to dream of a new creation where the basis of the suffering will no longer be. We need to dare to dream, even when the dreams appear too optimistic or even unrealizable. For without dreams we remain in the darkness of the hellish existence we are often condemned to. The dream is the spark that gives hope and the start of new life.

And so out of the suffering of my own people and experiences of the pain of some of the other peoples of the world who have also suffered margination, alienation, and rejection because of their racial or national background, I dare to dream of what could be and needs to be if humanity is to become a united family. Furthermore, I dare to dream of what could be because in many ways I have already seen it and have enjoyed the experience of this new creation, the enjoyment of the first buds of a new spring that promises a rich harvest. Something new is taking place in many regions of the world, like San Antonio. Could this be the beginning of

a breakthrough in personal, national, and international relations? The birth of a new humanity? How much further do
we have to go? Where is this new beginning taking us?

I have no formulated ideology or plan of action, neither
do I have any timetable of what will or must take place. I
am aware of the vast complexities of nationalistic and cultural identities. Yet I see things beginning to happen, as I
equally see profound obstacles to be worked through. Often ancient religious convictions make cultural adaptation
and transcultural love and fellowship next to impossible. Yet
breakthroughs are taking place. I dare to dream and hope of
what can be: that the human family might be one, rich in
the great diversity of the various nationalities of the world,
but no longer divided into enemies, free enough of racial and
cultural prejudices of the past to be able to love one another
as each is, free enough to learn from one another, free enough
to value and respect one another.

From Unsuspected Limitations to Unsuspected Richness

Even though I have always worked in San Antonio, my work
has taken me to other continents. I have circled the globe
several times and a bit of me has stayed in each place while
very much has become part of me. I have learned to be less
threatened by the differences of others, yet often I have been
challenged by them. In Rome several years ago, I was speaking at a meeting about development. An African was very
quick to challenge me. What I understood as "development"
actually had meant destruction for Africa and quite possibly for Americans as well, but we had never thought of it in
that way. Our development has meant drugs, alcohol, ner-
vous breakdowns, family breakdowns, a high percentage of
our citizens in jail, child suicide, destruction of nature, pol-
lution. The African challenged me: was this really human
progress or was it human destruction?

I have been in Latin America many times and I spent over a year in the Philippines, where I studied along with Asiatics from every country in Asia. Later on I spent time in India and East Africa. I went to Paris for studies and then to Rome to teach. Both in Paris and in Rome I had the opportunity not only of meeting local people but also of becoming good friends with people from other continents. I had the privilege of teaching in Australia, which is probably the most ethnically diverse country in the world. Furthermore, during the last ten years, I have consistently criss-crossed the U.S. to conduct workshops on intercultural questions. At the request of the Pentagon I worked with military personnel in Europe to assist them with similar problems. In all these experiences certain constants began to appear. A new world order is beginning to emerge. It is beyond Marxism or capitalism, it is beyond Roman Catholicism, Protestantism, or Islam. Something totally new is beginning to emerge.

As I have traveled around the world, I have become all the more aware of the uniqueness and richness of my own U.S./Anglo-Mexican/Latin identity. Yet I have equally become aware of our limitations. Every nationality and culture is a combination of wealth and poverty. Some have developed better in one way, while others in another. Those who appear to be poor and underdeveloped in the Western world are often very well developed in their ability to humanize. This is exemplified by vacation posters of the travel agents of the West. They entice the busy and often dehumanized executive to go to some far-off and "primitive" corner of the world to re-humanize. The so-called developed peoples teach others how to achieve results and even how to convert deserts into rich farmlands while the so-called primitive peoples are often masters in teaching others how to be human and not afraid of one's humanity. Both are needed for the total human enterprise to succeed.

My contact with others has helped me to become aware

of the limitations of my own way of life, yet they have not made me anti-American. In fact I appreciate more and more what the U.S. has to offer to its own people and to others. Yet the contact with others has kept me from sacralizing the culture of the U.S. as if it were perfect and without fault, without need of purification and redemption. I love my U.S. culture, but I refuse to adore it as if it were a god. I am comfortable and at home in it, but I am not blinded or enslaved by it. There are many aspects of it that need confrontation, challenge, questioning, reform, and repair if it is not going to self-destruct. Yet it is easy to be blinded by the glamor of abundance so that we convince ourselves that any invitation to change is a threat to our way of life.

The U.S.A. has a rich sense of discovery, risk, planning, organization, technology, efficiency, democracy, individual freedoms, while the Mexican way of life has a rich sense of family unity, friendship, spontaneity, humor, art, tradition, personal relations, pride, honor. Both traditions likewise have limitations. They can help one another so that both, without losing their innermost identity, can be improved and enriched. In some ways, this is already beginning to take place.

Within the U.S.A., it seems to me that the greatest force we are developing is not our high-powered weapons, technology, or economy, but our people force. Each day we receive many new immigrants into our land from throughout the world. Our country is rapidly becoming a multi-racial, multi-ethnic, and multi-lingual country united through a common spirit and a common language. Brown, white, black, and all the varieties of color in between are all becoming one family.

There is no doubt that there are problems and tensions, but the WASPish, monolingual image of the U.S. is rapidly giving way to the image of a multi-lingual mosaic of nations together making one great nation. This is not a confusing Tower of Babel, for the one language and the one common spirit of enterprise, liberty, and the quest of justice continue to be the fundamental uniting force of the various peoples who together make up this nation-culture. Ethnic festivals enrich the life of various of our large cities. Each cultural tradition brings something in while receiving much from what is already here. The U.S. way of life is not being destroyed. On the contrary, it is being greatly enriched. No one language, not even Spanish, is replacing English, yet other languages are frequently heard throughout the streets of the country. It is true that Spanish is rapidly becoming a second language, but far from being a threat to our national unity, it is opening the doors for commerce, international fraternity, and understanding of one another. This in itself is a new source of wealth.

A New Being: Universal and Local

I see two parallel forces at work throughout the world. They could easily appear contradictory, but in fact are quite complementary. Sometimes they appear to clash with the force of two strong and opposing currents of wind, but like the rain that follows such meteorological clashes, these collisions fertilize the local soil to produce new life.

On the one hand, the culture of modernity imposes itself upon all throughout the world with great and increasing momentum. Nothing will stop it. Wherever you go in the world, you can obtain Marlboro cigarettes, drink Coke, Pepsi, or Perrier, eat hamburgers out of plastic containers, buy Seiko watches or Japanese cameras, carry Adidas sacks, wear Levi blue-jeans and stenciled tee-shirts, brush your teeth with Colgate toothpaste, watch "Dallas" on TV, or hear the same Western rock music. Kids are playing the same electronic games in Paris as in San Antonio, Buenos Aires, Manila, and Bombay. Computerized machines dispense tickets at airports or railroad stations, give out information, and rapidly take over human jobs. We relate more with them than we do with other human beings. Computerese becomes the new universal language and whoever does not know it will be illiterate.

Satellite communications link the entire world, and we can all experience the events of the day as if they were taking place in our own city — whether a football match in Liverpool, the launching of a space rocket in Florida, the eruption of a volcano in Colombia, or race riots in South Africa. Common experiences, images, and information are quickly forming one common mentality throughout the world, while the local products that used to give each region its unique flavor and identity are rapidly being replaced by universal products easily found everywhere. The universal international markets are destroying the local identity of peoples and regions much faster and with much more planning than any immigrant would ever think of doing or would ever want to do. This is happening within the U.S. as rapidly as everywhere else in the world. We are developing a universal mind, universal flavors, universal clothing, universal tastes, universal rhythms.

Yet, there is another force at work: regional groups are resisting this totalizing absorption and reaffirming their local languages and traditions. It is as if there were a law of nature operating within the innermost drives of peoples that urges them to resist annihilation through universalization. They want to participate in the universal culture that is emerging without being consumed by it.

Not only are the Mexican-Americans of the Southwest insisting on being recognized and treated as full-fledged U.S.-Americans, but other groups are equally legitimizing and enjoying their own biculturality. No longer are they trying to wipe out all their ancestral traits. On the contrary, they are discovering a new pride in their foods, their music, their dress, their culture, their religious practices, and their language. People are discovering that they do not have to cease being who they are in order to become "good Americans." In fact, it is not only healthier but also more fun to reclaim our ancestral roots. This bicultural and often bilingual (and sometimes multi-cultural and multi-lingual) identity is radically new in U.S.A.-American culture, for previously you had to give up, totally wipe out, and completely forget your past — even change your name and your religion — in order to be fully accepted as a true "American." U.S.-Americanism is not disappearing, but it is radiating a new image and experiencing a new soul — no longer the face and voice of a soloist, but the countenance and heart of an entire symphony.

I have experienced a similar phenomenon in other parts of the world. For example, the indigenous peoples of the Americas are very rapidly entering into modern culture, but they are also becoming more and more appreciative of their own tribal ways and languages and finding new ways of keeping them alive. Life in the reservations no longer means being totally subjected to an outside "Indian agent." The pre-Columbian nations are discovering new life and vitality. The blacks in the U.S. are rediscovering their African roots and taking a new pride in their version of the English language.

During my year at the East Asian Pastoral Institute, I lived with people from throughout Asia and found that this phenomenon is also present in many other parts of the world. The universalizing force of modernity is giving new energy in the quest for survival of local and regional cultures and languages. The various islands of the Philippines insist on maintaining their own languages, and Tagalog was chosen as the national language. The Basques in Spain have insisted on preserving their ways and their language.

Throughout the world I have also observed a great quest to remain in contact with ancestral roots. There is a growing emphasis on regional foods, music, folklore, and tradition. In many ways the world is becoming bilingual and bicultural: people are at home in their own language and culture and equally at home in one of the dominant languages and the universal culture. This is certainly true when the theologians of the Third World countries meet. Since English and French have been chosen as the two common languages of our meetings, few of us speak our native language during the meetings. We have to be at least bilingual, knowing our own and one of the major languages. The monolingual, monocultural person will be out of touch with tomorrow's world.

Nature seems to demand differentiation but this does not have to be opposed to universalization. Whereas in the past we have thought of universal culture as a uniform culture, in the future we will begin to witness a world culture that will be at once universal and particular. This seems to me a very positive development in the humanizing pilgrimage of world society.

The more a universal, rootless culture spreads throughout the globe, the more we will seek to be in contact with our own space/culture. A truly humanizing universalization demands a geo-cultural differentiation. Without it, humanity will become bored and tired of being tightly self-contained. Humanity, if it is to survive, needs a new way of dealing with cultural differences. Herein lies the contribution of the *mestizo* of today: to show in one's person that racial and cultural mixture does not have to be destructive of cultural identity, but that it can even strengthen it.

Continued Migrations

The universalizing process of humanity will continue because migrations continue, and given the present-day structures of commerce they will not be stopped. Executives of multinational corporations travel throughout the world to open new markets for their products, while poor people from the Third World are brought into the industrial nations to perform the work that their own citizens do not want to perform.

But it is not the migration of the poor that poses a threat to local culture. The poor who migrate to the U.S. want more than anything else to become "good Americans." They do not want to change the nation-culture they struggled to get to. It is the migration of the rich that poses the greatest threat to local culture. For the rich take with them an apparently "better way of life" and set up their own structures. This disrupts local cultures by introducing a new image of what it means to be a good human being. This is what strikes most strongly at the roots of local culture.

The migration of retired U.S. citizens to Mexico is bringing about change in areas like Guadalajara, Lake Chapala, and San Miguel de Allende. These towns are rapidly becoming little islands of the U.S. way of life within Mexico and introducing new ways into some of the most beautifully traditional areas of Mexico. Their physical charm remains, but their living soul is rapidly becoming much more U.S. than Mexican. Yet the U.S. citizens who retire there also become Mexicanized, but to a much lower degree than the Mexicans there Americanize.

This Americanizing process within old Mexico is especially evident among the youth, who find the U.S. way of life very appealing. Discos appear quickly and U.S. dress and fast foods become the rule of the day. Curiously, the more they seem to "Americanize" the more they become anti-American, probably because the U.S. is proposed as an ideal that they know is impossible for them to obtain.

The same phenomenon is apparent in practically every large city in the world where the U.S. has personnel working and living with their families. The U.S. way of life is introduced to all the people as *the* way of life. Commercial enterprises quickly sell the trimmings of this way of life to the local people, thus enticing them to become "American," although simple economics make this next to impossible and U.S. immigration laws generally prevent it. Thus the love-hate relationship continues to develop and local cultures continue to be threatened. Their people are not allowed to migrate to the U.S., but the exterior trimmings of the U.S. way of life are sold to them and replace their own products.

To a slightly lesser degree I have experienced the same phenomenon in Spain, France, Germany, Holland, Italy, England, and Greece. The U.S. image of "the good life" quickly migrates throughout the world via travellers, movies, music, TV programs, games, and technology. U.S.-style fast foods replace the local restaurants. Meanwhile, in the U.S., the Japanese culture of production, with a strong paternalistic and family arrangement, challenges and sometimes takes over our previously unquestioned union-versus-management system.

There is a new type of colonizer who conquers, imposes, and dominates not through military conquest but through economics and the plastics of consumer culture. The executives of the transnational corporations with their teams and their families move into foreign countries and create new needs and desires, not only through the advertisements for their products but also with their personal way of life, which often appears to be superior and more developed than the local ways. The international economy depends upon the migration of new ideas, products, and personnel, since new markets need to be discovered and cultivated. The way of life of the Western world could not continue without the migration of its people and its products to the rest of the world.

As the rich and the powerful continue to migrate into the Third World, the poor of the Third World continue to migrate into the First World. They are left with no choice. I visit daily with people who have had to migrate to the U.S., some legally and some illegally. Every one of them would have preferred to stay at home, but starvation or political assassination would have been the consequence. They have gone through incredible experiences of danger, endurance, pain, and anguish to get to the U.S. It was not just a better salary that caused them to migrate, but the choice between life and death.

The industrialized world has created needs within the Third World. Now Third World people must find employment within the industrialized world and send money back to their families so that the Third World can pay the interest it owes to the industrialized world. There is no way Argentina, Brazil, or Mexico can pay off their debts without aid from the outside. They incurred the debt while the industrialized world was "helping" them to "develop." Western-type development has been very costly for the Third World and has often resulted in greater poverty for the masses who were already poor. Before, they were simply poor: now they are poor and dependent. If Mexico is to pay off merely the interest it owes to the U.S., every man, woman, and child would have to pay a tax of $1.20 per month. In a country where unemployment and subemployment are extremely high and inflation runs wild, this will never be possible. The young have no chance for employment or even for improvement. For many of them, migration is equivalent to life.

And Mexico is not the worst off among the nations of the world. The growing poverty, misery, and dictatorial violence in the Third World will continue to force the poor to take whatever chances are necessary to migrate into richer fields. And the quest for survival is much stronger than any human law against migration.

Furthermore, as much as the industrialized countries oppose new migrations of the poor into their countries, they themselves seek them out to come to do the work none of their citizens want to do. Today there are many unemployed in the U.S., especially Hispanic and black youth. Many of our own farmworkers are underpaid or forced to work under incredible conditions. Yet our Congress is seeking to pass legislation that would legitimate the importation of a farm labor force from Mexico to harvest the crops. Germany has a guest-worker program, and in France many foreigners are brought in to do the undesired work.

The poor who migrate into a richer nation do not pose a threat to the local culture. In fact, the very opposite is true. The threat is to their own self-image and cultural identity. They come because they want to better their lives. Thus they try to take on to themselves the traits of the host culture. The adults may fantasize about the great life in the old country, but the new generation often abhors their racial and cultural identity because of the ridicule they suffer at school, in the neighborhoods, and even in the churches. Everything in the new society makes the children feel different and odd. The dominant society quite naturally projects images of its own people as normative. Those who are different often experience a deep sense of shame and inferiority.

As the children grow up, they often strive to get rid of everything that in any way is linked to the old ways and take unto themselves the traits of the new culture. They will even make efforts so that their own children will not be "contaminated" with the language and cultural traits of the culture of the old country. Yet in time, the children of this first generation, who grew up totally in the new culture, sometimes reclaim the culture of their parents in a deeper and even more radical way. In many ways, though, they already belong to the new culture. It is here that the cultural *mestizaje* begins to emerge.

Mexican immigrants to the U.S. often want their children to become more U.S.-American than any native-born citizen. They do not want their children to have to suffer the insults and hurts they had to endure. But the culture of our parents is so deep that it is transmitted in an almost biological way. We can adjust to a new culture and even assume into ourselves many of the traits of the new culture we have moved into, but we can never totally cease being who we are.

New generations discover that certain aspects of their national and cultural identity are so much a part of their inner selves that they are not free to give them up. The new *mestizaje* occurs when they take unto themselves the new culture while combining it with their own inner selves. If they return to the ancestral home, they quickly discover that they are now foreigners in their own land for they have taken on the cultural personality of the new country. At first, this bicultural personality is difficult to live with, but in time it provides the basis for a new synthesis.

This new synthesis is easy to talk about, but it never takes place easily. There is first a deep and profound loneliness, the loneliness of not even being able to conceptualize and verbalize the reasons for the social alienation. Attempts will be made to "unbe" in order to be. Games will be played. The inner self will be suppressed into an almost total silence. Finally, through struggle and suffering the new identity will begin to emerge and the self will be able to shout out with joy: *"I am."* This new identity does not eliminate either the original culture of the parents or the culture of the new country. On the contrary, it enriches both by opening up each to the possibilities of the other.

Threshold of a New Humanity

When I first discovered our own *mestizaje,* I thought we were unique as a people. Yet as I started to study our ancient past, I discovered the rich mixtures that had formed the peoples who in turn had formed us. The ancient pre-Columbian nations had borrowed much from each other, and even though they existed as separate nations, they shared many traits in common. Our Spanish ancestors were themselves a rich mixture of the many peoples who had invaded the Iberian peninsula. The eight hundred years of Islamic rule had left its deep imprint in the Spanish soul. The people, the dances, the language, the music, the literature, and even our Catholic liturgy were enriched by elements received from Islamic culture. To this day, we use elements of the Mozarabic rite in our marriage ceremonies in our Hispanic Catholic churches.

Soon I discovered that Europe itself was such a rich mixture brought about through invasion, commerce, military occupation, and the transport of slaves. The idea of being "pure" seems to appear only when people forget their origins. All modern-day nations and cultures are products of a "mesticizing" process that often has long been forgotten.

With the beginning of the great European expansion in the late fourteenth century, a new and totally unprecedented stage in the evolution of humanity through *mestizaje* was opened. Europeans traveled, conquered, dominated, and gave birth to children among the local populations. Today the people of the former European empires and colonies are migrating to Europe and North America and taking their culture and language with them. In their new lands, they too are giving birth to new generations of children among the local populations.

Following the categories of Teilhard de Chardin, it seems that we are witnessing the birth of a new phylum of human life, the breakthrough to a truly human family. As in any breakthrough, it will not come about without much pain, suffering, turmoil, and confusion, for the introduction of something truly new is not easily understood or appreciated. In the past humanity has lived as tribes, as clans, as principalities, as city-states, and as nations.

But today there are too many forces and interests at work that totally bypass national boundaries and national concerns. Modern-day weapons make the concept of nation against nation, ideology against ideology, and even religion against religion a real threat to the whole of human existence. New forms of life must be found if humanity is to survive.

The new *mestizaje* that is taking place in diverse forms every place on the globe represents a breakthrough to a new humanity. Diversity in the various historico-geographical regions of the world will continue to be evidenced and even strengthened through the quest for roots and continuity with our ancestors. Yet there will also emerge a great common unity that we all seek but have not yet experienced. This new unity will not be homogeneity, a humanity without differences; it will be a new mosaic of the human race.

The Ultimate Mestizaje

Within Catholicism, Vatican Council II opened up a new era in our understanding and appreciation of other religions. Whereas before we had always seen ourselves as opposed to all others, the Council sought to discover and proclaim what we had in common and what could be the basis of a world family without everyone becoming Western and Catholic: "In her task of fostering unity and love among men, and even among nations, [the Church] gives primary consideration in this to what human beings have in common and to what promotes fellowship among them" (*Nostra Aetate,* no. 1).

Whereas in previous times many had simply seen other religions as the work of Satan and as errors that had to be eradicated, now the highest authority of the church stated:

> The Catholic Church rejects nothing which is true and holy in these religions.... Though differing in many particulars from what she holds and sets forth, they nevertheless often reflect a ray of that Truth which enlightens all men.... The Church has this exhortation for her sons: prudently and lovingly, through dialogue and collaboration with the followers of other religions, and in witness of Christian faith and life, acknowledge and preserve and promote the spiritual and moral goods found among these men as well as the values of their society and culture." (*Nostra Aetate,* no. 2)

In making these proclamations, the church returns to its original tradition of dealing with other religions as was evident in St. Paul, St. Justin Martyr, and other great Fathers of the church. Yet it was a tradition that had long been forgotten and replaced by the practice of opposing everything Catholic to everything non-Catholic — whether Protestant or of other religions. Thus the Council Fathers perceive and proclaim the gospel in its most dynamic and original way, no longer in terms of opposing peoples and their religions, but as the new unifying power capable of piercing through almost impenetrable boundaries and creating a new human fellowship. To many of us ordinary Catholics, this proclamation would not only have been unthinkable but would have sounded totally heretical before the Council. A Copernican revolution in our official outlook toward other religions and our relation to them had been officially proclaimed by our church.

The Council's decree on missionary activity (*Ad Gentes*) had some very important instructions for missioners:

> That they may be able to give this witness of Christ fruitfully, let them be joined to those men by esteem and love, and acknowledge themselves to be members of the group of men among whom they live. Let them share in the cultural and social life by the various exchanges and enterprises of human living. Let them be familiar with their national and religions traditions, gladly and reverently laying bare the seeds of the Word which lie hidden in them. (*Ad Gentes,* no. 11).

It is refreshing how the decree uses the model of Christ himself to provide a practical methodology for all missioners:

> Christ himself searched the hearts of men, and led them to divine light through truly human conversation.... Thus they themselves [Christ's disciples] can learn by

sincere and patient dialogue what treasures a bountiful
God has distributed among the nations of the earth. But
at the same time let them try to illumine these treasures
with the light of the Gospel to set them free and bring
them under the dominion of God their Savior.

(Ad Gentes, no. 11)

As the missionaries become members of the group they go to
serve and enter into true dialogue with them, they will never
cease being who they are culturally. Yet they will be changed
in such a profound way that they will feel like foreigners when
they return home for visits. They never fully become the
other, yet they become more and more foreign among their
own home people. Thus true missionaries become cultural
mestizos to be agents of fellowship among the various peoples
of the world.

The Council was very clear to state that missionaries do
not go to impose an old-world model of church, but to im-
plant the seeds of the gospel, which, in combination with the
local cultural soil, will give birth to a new local church:

The seed which is the Word of God sprouts from the
good ground watered by divine dew. From this ground
the seed draws nourishing elements which it transforms
and assimilates into herself. Finally, it bears fruit. This
is in imitation of the Plan of the Incarnation and thus
young churches, rooted in Christ, take unto themselves
in a wonderful exchange all the riches of the nations
which were given to Christ as an inheritance.

(Ad Gentes, no. 22)

These new churches will be no mere prolongations of the old
churches that begot them. There will be continuity, but there
will equally be newness. The response of faith will produce a

new people, and the people who respond in faith will produce a new church:

> From the customs and traditions of their people, from their wisdom and their learning, from their arts and sciences, these Churches borrow all those things which can contribute to the glory of their Creator, the revelation of the Savior's grace or the proper arrangement of Christian life. (*Ad Gentes,* no. 22)

It might be said that Vatican II brought to an end the long era of ecclesiastical fear of otherness, especially religious otherness. Before we were afraid of being contaminated by what appeared to us as the false religions of all non-Catholics. Now we were instructed to seek the good, the true, and the holy in other religions and to collaborate with them for the well-being of humanity. The proclamations opened the doors for previously unimagined possibilities.

We were told not to separate ourselves from others, but to mix lovingly with them and, in the very mixture, give witness of the universal love of Christ for all peoples. The Council did not call for a cultural *mestizaje* as such, but if we carry out its instructions, a cultural *mestizaje* will take place.

I suspect the deepest question, which we are even afraid to pose, is this: Is religious *mestizaje* possible? Given the fact that religion is the deepest and most unifying element of culture, can there be true cultural *mestizaje* without a corresponding religious *mestizaje?* I have no doubt that many would recoil at the thought of such a possibility. Yet can we speak of a true universal fellowship without addressing the question of religious *mestizaje?*

There is nothing that keeps people further apart than their religions. Young couples of two different religions — even within the family of Christian denominations — think that religion will not be an obstacle to their wedded life. They soon find out that it makes a great and profound difference. For religion gives us incredible bonds of solidarity as it sacralizes our differences. It is the ultimate root of our earthly existence and identity. Religion has been the cause of some of the bloodiest wars. It can be the deepest and strongest barrier to human unity.

Is religious *mestizaje* possible? Is that not the way Christianity has proceeded since the beginning? Did not Jesus, the Galilean whose parents had migrated first to Bethlehem, then to Egypt, and later back to Galilee, introduce radically new ideas to his own Jewish ways? And did not Paul confront Peter at Jerusalem to allow for a new cultural and religious synthesis for the Gentiles? And did not the Fathers of the church continue this process with the *sophia* of the Greek world? And so did Augustine in England, Boniface in Germany, Patrick in Ireland, and Cyril and Methodius for the Slavonic peoples. In fact Pope St. Gregory instructed Boniface: "The temples consecrated to idols should not be destroyed, but only the idols which are found within them. Prepare some holy water, sprinkle the interior and install altars and relics of the saints.... In this way this nation, seeing that their temples are not destroyed, will uproot the error from their hearts, will know and adore the true God, and will assemble in the places they are accustomed to." It was this type of evangelizing activity that allowed the various nationalities of the old continent to discover a new common and unifying element, while maintaining local identity and specific characteristics.

The gospel did not destroy any of the European nations, but it did give them a new way of living and relating to one another. Some of the great shrines of Christian Europe were built upon the foundations or walls of earlier pre-Christian temples. Many of the ancient religious rites and celebrations were assumed and incorporated into the Christian calendar and liturgy. This is what makes Europe so beautiful: a profound unity in the context of a very rich diversity. Today, we need to go even further.

Mexican *mestizaje,* although painful and negative at many moments of the process, can today play a positive role because its religious symbolism provides the synthesis of two apparently irreconcilable religions: Spanish Catholicism and the native American religions. The indigenous peoples of the Americas found the European religion incomprehensible, while the Catholic missioners found the native religions abominable. Yet in the brown Lady of Guadalupe, a new synthesis was achieved that was acceptable to both. I am convinced that were it not for the Lady of Guadalupe, there would be no Mexico today. There would simply be new Spain and the descendants of the native peoples, co-existing but never merging into one people. Had there been no religious *mestizaje,* the barriers between the two groups would still be insurmountable.

Mexican culture and Mexican Catholicism were born in the brown Virgin of Guadalupe. Mexican Catholicism cannot be adequately understood through the theological categories of Western Europe, for its indigenous substratum permeates every fiber of the Mexican church. Yet it is no mere syncretism. It is profoundly Christian, although its modes of expression have not always been recognized as legitimate by outsiders.

Today *mestizaje* is happening at all levels of human life, though rarely at the religious level, where it seems to be unthinkable for many. Yet it is precisely at this level that the greatest challenge for a united humanity presents itself. Jesus of Nazareth offers the world a true way of becoming a universal family without destroying the local genius or even the local religion of the people. Transformation yes, but destruction no. It was the migrant Jesus of Nazareth who had been raised in highly mesticized Galilee who prayed "that all might be one." From the personal experience of suffering rejection as a Galilean, he lived and proclaimed the Reign of God where all will be accepted and welcomed. It is from the bottom of society that a new universalism is introduced and offered.

Jesus invites all to a conversion from their old ways to the way of the love of God, neighbor, enemy, and one another. And who are neighbors? In the story of the Good Samaritan Jesus makes it clear: not necessarily those who share the same religion and the same culture, but those who act on behalf of the other in need. For Jesus, love of the other allows us to go beyond all our barriers and even transgress our religious taboos if necessary for the sake of the other in need. Jesus does not destroy religion but he does defy its sacralized and absolutized limitations and barriers. His only absolute is the universal love of all people.

In the conversion to the way of Jesus we are invited to enter into a new way of relating with others and with the ultimate other: all as children of the same God and brothers and sisters of each other. But we do not have to cease being who we are in order to enter into the new fellowship; we do not even have to give up our religion, but only live it in a radically new way. The Jews who followed Jesus continued being Jews, but they were now Jews in a radically new way. The Gentiles continued being Gentiles, but they were so in a radically new way. In conversion, their own socio-cultural identity, including its religious dimension, was not destroyed. What was destroyed was their exclusivity. The Jews as Jews and the Gentiles as Gentiles could now enter into a new fellowship together.

The radical universalizing newness of the way of Jesus of Nazareth is that it offers people the possibility of a hyphenated existence: Jewish-Christians, Gentile-Christians, Afro-Christians, Asian-Christians, *Mestizo*-Christians. Thus the way of Jesus affirms local identity while opening it up to fellowship and free exchange with all others. Jesus' way is the opposite of the abstract universals of philosophy or ideology; it is concrete, specific socio-cultural identity no longer threatened by others or afraid of being contaminated by others.

It is in opening up to others, with all the risks and possibilities involved, that the particular, without ceasing to be particular, now becomes universal. And we cannot open up to others without offering to them some of what we are and receiving from them some of what they are. Yet in this process no one ceases to be, but all are enriched. All have to die to their exclusivity, but no one will simply die. On the contrary, all will become richer in the process.

Will the great religions of the world, which are hesitant even to dialogue, ever be able to mesticize so as to produce the ultimate source of human unity? In some small ways this is beginning to happen. I have a good friend who is a Catholic priest/Buddhist monk. He says that his Buddhism has helped him to be a better Catholic and his Catholicism has helped him to be a better Buddhist. The Christian faith is being expressed through pre-Columbian rites and customs in many areas of Latin America, through the ancient African myths and rituals, and through the deeply mystical religious traditions of India. This process is slow, but it is indeed beginning and the results are as astonishing as they are promising. They are pregnant with possibilities for a new future, for a new creation. European and North American missioners who become involved in this process speak of how profoundly enriching it has been for them. As the gospel enriches peoples, the peoples enriched produce new and enriching expressions of the one gospel.

What the world needs today is a Guadalupe-event, an eruption in an unsuspected region of the world through the mediation of an unimagined person who offers the masses a new source of unity and hope. Eventually the great religions will join the people. I often ask myself if the liberation movements and their theological expression arising in various regions of the Third World will not provide the new Guadalupe-event that will unify apparently irreconcilable forces. The new universal language of the religious thinkers and leaders of much of the Third World is that of liberation theology with its emphasis on the God of people, the historical process, the local identity of the reflecting community, and a universal concern for the poor, the outcasts, and the needy of the world.

This new universal/particular existence is already beginning. What do we do with it? How do we situate ourselves within it? It is not easily understood, often it is not suspected, and frequently it is greatly feared. It is our challenge to help bring new order out of the present-day chaos, new meaning out of the present-day confusion, new hope out of the present-day fears, new joy out of the present-day tensions. Modern-day weapons of war coupled with national, cultural, ideological, and religious division could easily destroy humanity, but a new universal fellowship based on respect for others, mutuality of existence, and free exchange of all that we are will allow humanity not only to survive but to live in that peace that we all desire.

The challenge is not easy, but it is fascinating. The risks are great, but so are the stakes. Given the present situation of our planet, the option is between annihilation or survival. No wall or immigration law will lock in or keep out any people. The necessities and possibilities of migration increase at all levels. Our challenge is to make it positive and radically new.

This new humanity is emerging in the middle of the American continent. The old Nordic cultures of Europe, which formed the cultural/religious base of the U.S.A., are meeting and merging with the Latin *mestizo* cultures of the old Iberian world, which mesticized with the native nations of the Americas. In the borderlands between the U.S.A. and

Mexico, peoples who have never really met before are today meeting one another, intermingling, and becoming a new and united people. Differences are not being destroyed, but they are being transcended and celebrated as together we usher in the beginning of the new race of humanity. We are on the way, that all might truly be a united family of the planet earth.

Epilogue

A Reflection Twelve Years Later

From within my own personal experience and that of a growing number of *Frontera Mestizos* of the United States,[1] I am more convinced than ever before that in our flesh and blood, in our music and art, in our dances and poetry, in our murals and novels, our foods and our marriages, our struggles and our dreams and most especially our Mestizo babies and youth, we Mestizos are anticipating the new humanity of the third millennium. As more and more cultures meet and encounter one another, it becomes evident that the future is indeed mestizo, but what kind of mestizaje will we produce?

Precisely in the context of the increasingly violent ethnic-racial and religious wars of the present moment, mestizaje appears as the only way of piercing through the impenetrable walls of distrust and hatred of others which have produced so much bloodshed in the past and are destroying humanity today. It can be the guarantee not only of the survival of humanity, but even more so the irruption of a new humanity which will be a family made up of all the peoples of the world — not without serious birth-pains and even more powerful pains of growing up, but nevertheless a truly new being on the face of the earth. Together combinations, none of the ancient roots fading out completely, a new planetary humanity is in the making. What a blast! But for this to happen, we must take an honest look at the reality of mestizaje: how it has functioned in the past and how it can function today.

With this in mind, and knowing of my own efforts to deal with the reality of my American-Mexican mestizaje in my doctoral dissertation (published as *Galilean Journey: The Mexican American Promise*), a French couple who had adopted African children who in turn had married into French families urged me to explore the dynamics of my own experience so as to help others see their own reality in a new and exciting way. This gave rise in 1984 to the preparation and publication of *L'avenir est au Métissage*, which was prefaced by none other than Léopold Sédar Senghor, the noted father of Black thought (*père de la Négritude*) and member of l'Académie Française. In that preface he stated that "The great merit of this work is not that it announces that the future is mestizo but that it demonstrates its overall success. . . . One cannot think of a better way of defining the universal civilization of the future than through a universal mestizaje."

The work was quickly translated into English. Over the past twelve years, *The Future Is Mestizo: Life Where Cultures Meet* has been republished several times and has been used in many classrooms not only in the United States, but also in many other parts of the world. Businessmen, professionals and civic leaders have found it as revealing of the depth of our expanding *frontera-Mestizo* reality as have religious thinkers and social scientists.

Many who have read it have expressed gratitude for having been able to appreciate the dynamics of what is taking place within their own lives. These positive comments have come not only from my own Mexican-American people, but also from many others of different ethnicities, especially African-Americans and Asian-Americans. Some have expressed that the book was a real inner liberation for them, others expressed that it was a source of spiritual healing, while still others saw it as providing a realistic and optimistic guide for the new humanity of the third millennium. Senghor stated: "here we discover a new language and a new vision of dealing with the oldest problematic of humanity." I have been most edified, humbled, and grateful for all these marvelous comments.

When it was first published twelve years ago there was hardly any literature in the United States that spoke about the mestizaje process within our country. Richard Rodriguez had just published his *Hunger for Memory*, which appeared as a painful but very real rejection of mestizaje as experienced by many of the Hispanics in the United States. Today, there is growing body of knowledge not only in the United States but also abroad. In 1995, Patricia Schutz presented a fascinating thesis at the University of Metz, France, on the evolution of the term and its usage in the Franco-Germanic border as reflective of the social status of the reality. In 1997, Gil Pereira of Brazil produced a breakthrough work in the Afro-Brazilian mestizaje at the University of Montreal. In 1999, CONCILIUM, the international journal of theology, published a number on mestizaje through the prism of "the transgression of borders."

By far the deepest and most creative European work on mestizaje was published by Professor Jacques Audinet in 1999 under the title *Le Temps du Métissage*. It is a monumental work on the intrinsic relationship between mestizaje, new civilizations, and democracy.

Within the United States, new works began to expand the theme. *San Martin de Porres*, the doctoral thesis of Alejandro Garcia Rivera, studies it through a process of semiotic analysis. Roberto Goizueta has explored the "Cosmic Race" theory of Vasconcelos. Jeanette Rodriguez's book *Our Lady of Guadalupe* explores the theme through the experience of Mexican-American women. Arturo Bañuelas' book *Mestizo Christianity* pulls together the various writings of Hispanic mestizo theologians of the United States. Lionel Sosa's book *The Americano Dream: How Latinos Can Succeed in Business and Life* explores the issue as it works out in business and professional life. Richard Rodriguez's latest article in *Harpers Weekly*, "Mix Blood," is a marvelous development of his own dealings with mestizaje as the way of ultimate survival.

The Future is Mestizo was produced during my first year as Rector of San Fernando Cathedral in 1984. Since then, my own fascination with the positive results of the ongoing mestizaje in every domain of human life has continued to increase. I could see it happening in every level of life, and as I was baptizing new mestizo children and guiding them through the process of religious education, I could not help wonder at the combinations which produced such beautiful children. Out of this experience came *Our Lady of Guadalupe: Mother of the New Creation* and *San Fernando Cathedral: Soul of the City* (co-authored with Timothy Matovina), which continue to explore the theme of religious mestizaje — a theme that fascinates me more and more and whose urgency becomes more and more apparent.

The deepest and most moving exploration of the mestizo journey from its roots in ancient Mexico, through modern-day Mexico to Texas is John Philip Santos' *Places Left Unfinished at the Time of Creation* (1999). John Philip's own family had deep roots in the American-mestizo experience of San Fernando, and our conversations over the years have constantly brought to light new aspects of mestizaje that we had never suspected. John Philip and his brothers George and Charles are marvelous examples of the positive potential of the American-Mexican mestizaje — all three very Mexican while at the same time being very American! They love who they are, are grateful to their parents, and have become eminently successful in the United States in media, medicine and the arts.

I was deeply touched when my good friend Professor Davíd Carrasco of Princeton brought up the idea of revisiting *The Fu-*

ture is Mestizo, which he called illuminating, prophetic and visionary. John Philip Santos, Sandra Cisneros, Henry Cisneros, Raul Yzaguirre, Lionel and Kathy Sosa, Al and Gisella Aguilar, Mario and Ellen Garcia, and many other friends also urged me to revisit and expand the original work. Former students and now colleagues Tim Matovina, Roberto Goizueta, and Alex Garcia Rivera have consistently urged me to do some more work on this topic. So I am most grateful that Professor Carrasco and novelist Sandra Cisneros agreed to help in the expansion of this work.

In conversations with these close friends for whom the topic of mestizaje holds a growing fascination, we agreed that given the growth of ethnic gangs, ethnic-racial rivalry, ethnic "cleansing" wars, and the growth of racist hate groups, the topic of a new paradigm for true human unity was urgent and crucial. The present-day multicultural model of society is a good step forward, but it doesn't touch the roots, inner dynamism, or invisible forces of what is taking place not just in the frontera between Mexico and the United States but throughout the world. Professor Audinet sees mestizaje as the natural by-product of true democracy.

Without a new way of viewing and understanding the human family in its unstoppable process of becoming, ethnic or racial groups will easily and quickly destroy not only one another, but humanity as a whole. As the world becomes more crowded, the battles for space will become more intense. This is the thesis in Samuel P. Huntington's much-debated article "The Clash of Civilizations" (*Journal of Foreign Affairs*), in which he states that the ultimate war which will destroy humanity will be a religious-ethnic war. The efforts at "ethnic cleansing" going on around the world have potential to destroy the entire human race. Beyond the misery of famine that is devastating Africa, their ethnic-tribal wars are even most destructive; beyond the 500 years of oppressive servitude, the recent genocide of the Mayan Indians by the Guatemalan military (aided by the United States) was a bloody holocaust; beyond the crucified existence of the dark-skinned Latin American poor, the efforts of American border patrols to keep them away from the "Promised Land" cries to God for justice. In spite of the declaration of the basic rights of human beings and all the efforts at multicultural harmony, ethnic-racial tensions continue to appear, increase in intensity, and tear people apart. These tensions can potentially destroy everyone. New ways must be found beyond the present day's models of human existence if humanity is to survive.

The more we talked and explored the destructive status of our world, the more we became convinced that our frontera mestizaje was the greatest thing we had to offer the human family! Not the mestizaje of Latin America, which had produced such a deep sense of shame in everything Indian and such an exaggeration of the value of everything European, but the new mestizaje that we Hispanics are discovering and elaborating here in the United States — one that joyfully reclaims the heritage of all our parents, grandparents, and ancestors. A denial of — or even worse, a shame of — one side of one's heritage is a life of eternal self-torture and self-destruction. A reclaiming and restructuring is a life of freedom and creativity. We long to introduce this mestizaje to others and offer its fascinating benefits for humanity. We reject as harmful to everyone any type of mestizaje that would attempt to deny one of the parent lines while extolling the other as the only way of being a true, a good, and a beautiful human being.

Like many other authors I know, I don't like to read my own works after they have been published. It is certainly not that I am ashamed of them or that I have changed my mind. It is just that once it is published, it seems that it no longer belongs to me, but to the reader! So I haven't read this little book of mine since it was published.

As I read the book for the first time in twelve years, there were many emotions going through me. The most consistent one was awe! Did I really write all this good stuff? From where did I get this profoundly moving expression? Forgive me if I sound arrogant, but the simplicity and depth of the book is awesome! Being a man of faith, I could only thank God for having moved me to put these insights in writing. As I reread my own work of twelve years ago, I must confess that I am more convinced of the ideas presented in the book than ever before. Yet it is only a primer, only a beginning of what needs to be explored at far greater depth.

One of the areas which was not emphasized enough in my book and which needs to be explored at greater length is the negative aspects and consequences of mestizaje. In rereading *The Future Is Mestizo*, I realized that because my own process of mestizaje, even though it was quite painful at times, has nevertheless resulted in such an exciting and positive experience, I did not dwell sufficiently with the negative and soul-destructive aspects of the medieval mestizaje of Spain, the mestizaje of Latin America and of our own mestizaje process within the United States. When mestizaje takes place in the context of one parent group denying equality or even worse, the basic right to existence, of the other parent group — such as happened in the religious-racial, Christian-Jewish mestizaje of Spain of the fourteenth and fifteenth centuries — the mestizos become even the executioners of the branch of their people of which they hope to cleanse themselves. Such was the case of the first Grand Inquisitor, Tomás de Torquemada, who led the way in the "purity of blood" campaign of Spain, which resulted in the massacre of thousands of Jews and the expulsion of many more. He even declared Jewish-Christian marriages to be a capital offense. All this to try to cleanse himself of his old Jewish heritage — it was rumored that his grandmother had been a Jewish convert to Catholicism.[2]

The origins of *The Future Is Mestizo* were not academic research, philosophical inquiry or ideological speculation, but rather a prolonged journey into my own inner space and that of my people, which I had explored in *Galilean Journey: The Mexican American Promise*. I had many good guides to help me through this uncharted voyage to the innermost center of my earth, of my existence. Guides such as Jacques Audinet and Abel Pasquier from France, Francisco Aguilera from Mexico, Jesus Chavarria from California, Alfonso Nebreda from Japan, and John Linskens from Holland offered illuminating guidance along the way, but it was the stories and memory of my own people, the people from my *barrio*, from my father's grocery store, and my home parish in San Antonio who offered the greatest insights. Beyond all this, it was through gospel-reading, prayer, creative silence, and contemplation that this book came together. It was through the life-journey of the rejected Jesus the Galilean who had become the beginning of a new creation that my own mestizo journey took on a fantastic new meaning and mission. He was the key which unlocked the doors into many unsuspected chambers of new understanding, appreciation and insight.

At times the journey was painful, at times it was joyful and exciting. Sometimes it seemed to be leading nowhere, while at other times it was like discovering new heavens and new earths. New scars were frequently exposed, but healing was also gradually taking place. It seemed that the deeper I traveled into my own inner soul and that of our people, the greater freedom I experienced and the more creative I became, for in reaching for our roots I was actually reaching for God; in touching the ultimate in me, I was touching the ultimate that is God! What a trip!

The fact of mestizaje is happening everywhere and in many diverse ways. In fact, it has been taking place since the beginning of humanity, since Adam and Eve mated and produced their first child — a product of two diverse and distinct human beings. As Neal Ascherson brings out in his beautifully written *Black Sea*, new civilizations emerge as individuals, armies, and peoples dare to cross uncrossable frontiers and in the encounter not only are changed themselves, but also produce something truly new.

Without mestizaje producing encounters, humanity would most probably still be living in tribal villages collecting berries or simply hunting and fishing. Even when high civilizations are developed, once they isolate themselves from interchange — the Great Wall of China, for example — decay starts to set in. Though interchange is never without risks of undesirable elements, the greatest risk would be to prohibit any type of interchange at all! Interchange is an important vehicle for humanity to advance. The problem with mestizaje has never been biological or cultural but social. The great historical heresy of humanity has been the thought that one had to be a pure blood — that one could isolate oneself from the influence and impact of others. Thus the mestizo, the new child who guarantees the future, has been deemed as impure and unworthy, as a threat to the very life of both of the parent groups. Mestizo children are often considered as "sellouts" by both of the parent groups that produced them.

Jacques Audinet furthers this theme historically, politically and socially in his masterful work *L'temps du métissage*.[3] Whether mestizaje had been prohibited, tolerated, or commanded, it has taken place throughout history. One simply cannot understand the great human adventure without a grasp of the mestizo process that has accompanied human history since the beginning. Unlike the obligatory mestizaje of Alexander the Great, or the mestizaje through rape which gave rise to the Latin American mestizaje, today no one is forcing it, planning it or promoting it, but it is taking place at a faster pace than ever before.

Free intermarriage is on the rise everywhere. Mestizo children of all possible varieties are appearing everywhere and demanding to be recognized as such. Tiger Woods, one of the most popular athletes in the world, refuses to identify himself as just black, for he proudly recognizes that he is a mixture of Caucasian, black, Indian and Asian.[4] A few years ago, *Time* magazine produced a classical issue on "The New Face of America" — which was a multi-racial and multi-ethnic face! In 1997,

Newsweek published an issue on "The German Melting Pot"[5] — a long way from the "pure" Aryan race. The 1996 Multiracial Solidarity March in Washington, D.C., American multiracial citizens called for a multiracial designation on the 2000 census. More and more articles are referring to the growing mixtures of races and cultures throughout the planet, but especially in the United States.

I have presided at a growing number of interracial and interethnic marriages and have witnessed the beauty of their children — the body spontaneously picks up the best of both. But does the mind, the heart, the spirit and the soul? Does the mind and the heart refuse to value what the body has produced? The good that the body so naturally produces must be recognized and celebrated by the heart and the mind. The split between the biological and the social — the biological producing something beautiful while the mind produces a stigma that will mark the innermost soul of the Mestizo body as impure, contaminated, and inferior — is one of the greatest problems facing the new generations that are now coming into being.

But who is talking about it? Who is helping to clarify what is taking place within the hearts and minds of the Mestizo children who are suffering with deep-rooted complexes of inferiority because they are "different," of the Mestizo professionals still struggling to be something other than what they truly are, of the Mestizo entertainers still trying to emulate their Anglo-American counterparts while ignoring their own greatest potential, of religious people still trying to cleanse themselves of what one of the parent groups sees as the pagan and unworthy practices of the other?

Is religion or education helping? I don't think so. I do not believe people in religion or education have yet gone beyond the Anglo-American models of human existence. The churches generally want to convert us away from ourselves so as to become Anglicized while educators tell us about the people we are not while seldom introducing us to ourselves. There is room for "others," whether Asians, Africans, Native Americans, or Latino mestizos, to the degree that they can cease being "other" and become like the mainstream in every way. But this is not possible for those of us who biologically and spiritually were created different. Even plastic surgery cannot totally reconstruct anyone to really be other than they are!

While universities are still promoting departments of Black Studies, Chicano Studies, Latino Studies, Multiculturalism and the like, is anyone at all organizing departments of Mestizaje? Exploring the implications, the literature, the process, the psychological-social problems involved, the potential for humanity? Are doctoral theses and research projects being dedicated to this growing reality?

While religion is promoting "inculturation," none of the religious groups I know are dealing with the issues on the growing intercultural reality that is rapidly emerging through the process of mestizaje. This could be the greatest contribution and challenge of the churches as they baptize the new mestizo children into the family of their churches. Does the church really want them and value them as they are — as the carriers of the various races and ethnicities of their parents and grandparents?

Mestizaje will never be a positive process unless we are able to recognize that in the very difference there is beauty, honor, and prestige. This is the beginning of the inner freedom to be oneself. In the very blending of the differences into a new whole, everyone can be enriched, can become more human, and I dare to say, can become more divine. Each one of us individually, and each ethnic and racial group, radiates a bit of the glory of God and together, blending and sharing, we radiate much more of the infinite glory of God our creator.

Yet for this to take place, each one of us must know and appreciate ourselves as we truly are — neither inferior nor superior to anyone else, but definitely special and unique. This means that we have to learn the stories of our ancestors, the history of our past civilizations, the history of struggles, of our successes and failures, of our oppressions and exploitations. We have to learn about the art and literature of our ethnic ancestors, the beauty of their linguistic expression, the richness of their humor, and the depth of their religious practices. We must enter into their souls through their foods, celebrations and festivals. We can appreciate their social world through their folk wisdom and home life. We have to know our heroes and villains and visualize their faces and bodies, for it is through the body that primary revelation takes place. And most of all we must forgive those who have wronged us if we are to be released from their claws and obtain the inner freedom we need to move ahead with the new creation.

I have a very positive and realistic concept of mestizaje because I was fortunate to grow up in a family that was very proud of everything Mexican while being very excited about the freedom and opportunities of the American way of life. We were happy and proud to be both Mexican and American, hence we grew up seeking the best of both. My father was very Mexican, but hated the Mexican political and economic system and even more so the Mexican culture of peonage and racist-classist distinctions. He loved the possibilities of the United States, but hated what he considered the overly materialistic and individualistic spirit of the culture. My parents, from the earliest moments of my life, taught us to discern and pick the best of both — a winning combination. We were happy and proud to be a rich and exciting combination of both. We felt that being Mexican in the United States was the greatest thing possible; I still feel that way today. It's a great combination that is pregnant with creative possibilities.

Without a good knowledge and appreciation of ourselves as the unique persons that history, biology and geography have made us to be, we will have nothing to offer others. We will simply dissolve into a tasteless melting pot while never being fully accepted by a mainstream that will always find ways of reminding us we are different! We might be of a slightly different color or size and shape, but we would cease to be a unique people. We would live in the social vacuum of non-existence and hence in the permanent category of never fully belonging, always playing the games of trying to be someone we are not while hiding something that we are. In trying to be "just like the others" we really become nobody. We would become a people without an identity, without a place in the human family. This is devastating.

For the mestizaje to be positive, we must know and admire the heritage and language of our parents and their ancestors. But even when the language is no longer accessible, their cultures still flow within our veins. The blood memory continues to flow over countless generations. It may not always be very obvious, but it is always there, deeply buried in our subconscious. Without a conscious appreciation, one will always live in the shame of trying to hide, ignore, cleanse, purify away that side of one's parentage one is ashamed of! Ignorance or shame of the story and ethnic identity of one's parents is self-destructive.

The Negative

Biologically, mestizaje is an enriching of the genetic pool and therefore very positive. "Pure" groups tend to weaken and transmit their weakest traits to future generations. Culturally, mestizaje is the creative birth of new forms of language, art, foods, music, and even religious expression. But sociologically, mestizaje can be very destructive, as was the case in Latin America, where the Native American side of us was looked down upon as inferior, ugly, backward, ignorant, and destined to serve the white European masters, who alone were seen as fully human. The mestizo children were looked down upon and considered unwanted by both parent groups.

Mestizos had no social space they could call their own or be among their own, for they were always marginalized from the mainline space of their parent groups. This was the beginning of the deep sense of alienation, loneliness, and inferiority. This was the beginning of the dark and silent night of the Mestizo soul — nowhere did it belong, nowhere did it find peace and tranquility, nowhere was there anyone around who could understand. Masks, quiet rage, and inner silence seemed the only way of survival.

The dominant and powerful who themselves had initiated the process of mestizaje failed to recognize the beauty of this new human reality. This has been the great failure and impoverishment of Latin American societies. This is where the very progenitors of the greatest mestizaje the world has ever known failed — and I would even say betrayed — their own children, their own progeny. Rather than being proud, they have treated their own creation with disdain. They have not appreciated their own greatest treasure and contribution to the future of the human family.

The dominant societies created, believed, and imposed the image of the inferior, ugly, pagan, and backward native. This produced a deep existential shame that unfortunately continues to be promulgated by modern media and Western religious groups of every denomination. This shame in our Native American parentage produced a very painful destructive psychosis. This deep sense of shame and existential inferiority became a disabling ingredient of mainstream Latin American culture. Out of this emerged a perpetual sense of alienation and non-belonging — neither Spaniard nor Native American. It forced the mestizo to put on many masks and assume many personalities. Authenticity appeared impossible and undesirable if one wanted to fit into the dominant-elite European culture and society. This has been the psychological poison that has kept the Latin American Mestizo from a radical acceptance and appreciation of the Mestizo identity and role in forging a new civilization.

Out of this pain of margination and shame, the Latin American mestizo strove to become more European than any European while treating the Natives even worse than the worst of the European masters! They more than anyone else tended to deny the value of anything indigenous. They had to be better than the Europeans in everything — including the bad treatment of the Indians! It should come as no surprise that when the movements of liberation started, the movement to claim our own innermost identity, the efforts have rejected not only the European background, but even all mestizaje. They saw the mestizo as the greatest and innermost enemy of the indigenous people — enough of one to be able to destroy them from within, and sufficiently European to be even more cruel than the European masters. They could never become the interlocutors between the two groups because they were denied authenticity by both.

This same negative process is happening in the United States when Hispanics who are interiorly ashamed of their *Hispanidad* end up treating fellow Hispanics in a worse way than any mainline person would do, while at the same time being more "gringo" than anyone else. Why are they ashamed? For many reasons. We are never taught our history, so it seems that we are a people without a history. We never hear about our heroes, only about our gangsters. Our language is questioned and ridiculed both in the United States and in Latin America. While many mainline persons are trying to learn Spanish, many of our Hispanic parents try to keep their children from speaking Spanish, thus giving them a sense of backwardness if they speak Spanish. We are generally absent from the media, except when we appear as criminals, drug addicts, welfare recipients and the like. The public image of Hispanics in the United States still, in spite of the many advances, continues to be very negative, including our image on Hispanic language television, magazines and radio. The dark-skinned Hispanic is hardly ever present except in very subservient roles. No wonder that children growing up in these circumstances develop such a deep shame in the Latino heritage that runs in their veins, colors their skin and animates their spirit. No wonder they try in many ways to exorcise the *Hispanidad* out of their veins and souls!

The Challenge

The great challenge today is to transform the destructive sense of mestizo shame into a life-giving sense of pride and excitement. This happened during one of my classes at the University of California at Santa Barbara when one of my students exclaimed: "I never imagined it was so exciting to be Latino!" while a non-Latino in the class stated "I feel cheated — why has all this beauty been kept hidden from the rest of us?"

Our Hispanic advertisers throughout the United States are truly on the way to using the popular media and the quest to sell products to Hispanics to bring about this transformation. Through their advertisements, they are creating a new social awareness of the richness and beauty of our emerging American Latino mestizaje. Our storytellers such as Rodolfo Anaya, Sandra Cisneros, Victor Villaseñor, and John Philip Santos are writing with great depth, illuminating humor, and graceful pride about our people. Our artists and songwriters are helping us and others to experience the beauty and excitement of being Mestizo-American.

This transformation from disabling shame to energizing pride will come about as we convert the sense of margination and non-belonging into one of new being, new potential, and new life. The Mestizo is the product of two civilizations and lives equally between the mainline existence of both. Mestizos are part of both while not being exclusively either. I am very "gringo" in Latin America while being very "Mexican" in the United States, but I am not two persons, I do not act differently in Mexico or the United States. Yet in neither am I ever considered simply one of the group. I am always both keen and foreigner at the same time. This "in-between" is the pain and the potential, the suffering and the joy, the confusion and the mystery, the darkness and the light of Mestizo life. As I claim this ambiguity and recognize it for what it truly is, I become the bearer of a new civilization that is inclusive of all the previous ones. No longer do I carry the burden of shameful news but rather become the bearer of the good news of the future that has already begun in us. The pain, confusion, and darkness of the past give way to healthy excitement, new knowledge, and creative imagination. This is exciting! It is exhilarating! It is energizing.

This very "in-between," far from being negative, has a tremendous advantage. I am an inside-outsider of both and thus have the ability of knowing both from within and from the outside. I can know them in ways they can never know me or even suspect! I can truly become the interlocutor who will help both to see and appreciate themselves and each other in ways they had never before suspected. I can become infinitely more creative, for I have more cultural worlds within me than anyone who is a descendent of only one culture. I can also promote the dignity and welfare of my oppressed indigenous parents, as I can help to purify the oppressive elements of the foreigners who took over. I am both, and also something new. I can even have more fun, for I can party in many more ways than imagined by any one group alone.

Furthermore, as the mestizo "in-between" keeps expanding, as the "frontera" keeps expanding both north and south at the same time, it keeps including more and more peoples, ethnicities, and races. The mestizo existence is by its very historical nature and origins a radical biological, cultural, and spiritual openness to others — no matter who they are. It is the biological-spiritual opposite of ethnic and racist boundaries. In fact, it is the deepest and most far-reaching transgression of ethnic and racial laws of segregation.

Biologically and culturally, mestizaje is an important process in the evolution of the human race into a truly human family — from divided and fighting tribes, clans, nations, and races to a united human family. What needs to change radically is the social appreciation of mestizaje from that of being a pariah to that of being a gift. Our great challenge today is to introduce others to the excitement and potential of mestizaje. It is not a threat to anyone, but a contribution for everyone. A positive mestizaje will be the guarantee of the future of humanity, not just of any humanity, but a new humanity that will truly be a family made up of all the peoples of the world. What a blast.

Looking back from the present moment of time and space, I dare to say that the reflection upon our common journey as Mexican Americans has led to a new understanding for today and a creative vision for the future. Out of our suffering and struggles of the past comes not cynicism, fatalism and despair, but creativity, hope and expectation. This is truly energizing! And great fun.

We are truly in the springtime of a new humanity — a newness that is within our bodies and souls, a newness that we wish to share with others who we hope will become part of this common journey of humanity. For within our mestizaje bodies the veins of all the human groups of the earth are already blending to produce new bodies, but it is our privilege and challenge to create the new soul that will animate this new body of humanity. I hope and pray that we can live up to this fascinating opportunity.

Notes

1. By *Frontera Mestizos* I refer to anyone born, growing-up and/or living within the greater USA–Mexican borderlands who biologically and/or culturally finds themselves to be a blend of the peoples of The USA and of Mexico.

2. Victor Perera, *The Cross and the Pear Tree: A Sephardic Journey*, Berkeley: University of California Press, 1995, p. 53.
3. Jacques Audinet, *Le Temps du Métissage*, Paris: Les Editions de L'Atelier, 1999, especially Chapter 5, pp 71–84.
4. John Leland and Bregory Beals, "In Living Colors" in *Newsweek*, May 5, 1997.
5. Andrew Nagorski, "The German Melting Pot" in *Newsweek*, April 21, 1997.